Also by Terry Ravenscroft

STAIRLIFT TO HEAVEN
STAIRLIFT TO HEAVEN 2 - FURTHER UP THE
STAIRLIFT
STAIRLIFT TO HEAVEN 3 - ALMOST THERE
STAIRLIFT TO HEAVEN 4 - STILL HANGING ON
CAPTAIN'S DAY
FOOTBALL CRAZY
IT'S NOT CRICKET!
JAMES BLOND - STOCKPORT IS TOO MUCH
INFLATABLE HUGH
I'M IN HEAVEN
THE RING OF THE LORD
SERIAL KILLER
DEAR PEPSI-COLA
DEAR AIR 2000
SAWYER THE LAWYER
LES DAWSON'S CISSIE AND ADA
THE RAZZAMATAZZ FUN EBOOK
ZEPHYR ZODIAC
CALL ME A TAXI
GOOD OLD GEORGE!
DEAD MEN DON'T WALK

Much of this book was previously published under the title of Dear Customer Services.

All the letters to the food and drink companies and their letters to me are entirely genuine. Not a word, including the spelling and grammar mistakes, has been altered.

T Ravenscroft (Mr) would like to thank the food and drink companies and their staff who replied to his letters, often with patience above and beyond the call of duty, and without whom this book would not have been possible. He would especially like to thank the Coca-Cola Company for the use of the name of their incredibly popular drink for the title of the book.

DEAR COCA-COLA

A RAZZAMATAZZ PUBLICATION

About the author

The day after Terry Ravenscroft threw in his mundane factory job to become a television comedy scriptwriter he was involved in a car accident which left him unable to turn his head. Since then he has never looked back.

Before they took him away he wrote scripts for Les Dawson, The Two Ronnies, Morecambe and Wise, Alas Smith and Jones, Not the Nine O'Clock News, Ken Dodd, Roy Hudd, and several others. He also wrote the award-winning BBC radio series Star Terk Two.

Born in New Mills, Derbyshire, in 1938, he still lives there with his wife Delma and his mistress Divine Bottom (in his dreams).

17 Lingland Road
New Mills
CHESHIRE

28th April

Coca-Cola and Schweppes Beverages
Uxbridge

Dear Coca-Cola

Coca-Cola is by far the favoured drink in our household, whether guzzled in vast quantities by my three sons, consumed in the diet version by my wife, or drunk freely by myself - albeit generally with a generous measure of rum in it. We rarely imbibe in anything else as I have always encouraged my family to drink it ever since I was witness to a demonstration in which an old coin had been left in a glass of Coca-Cola only to emerge twelve hours later looking as though it were brand spanking new. I thought to myself at the time 'If Coca-Cola can clean up an old coin like that, just think what a wonderful job it will do of keeping my intestines clear,' and my family and I have been drinking it ever since.

What I particularly like about Coca-Cola is that it is so consistent. What you see is what you get, as they say. And as I was only remarking the other day to a chap at the dentists where I'd taken two of my sons - Henry to have a couple of teeth out and Marcus for twelve fillings - 'Thank God there is one drink on the market that you can depend on.'

Could I ask a favour of you? We will shortly be having friends visit us for a few days and they are very strict vegetarians. Coca-Cola will be available to them by the bucketful of course, but naturally I wouldn't like to offer them anything which might be at odds with their vegetarian beliefs. I am of course aware that the recipe of Coca-Cola is a closely-guarded secret, and justly so, but with the above in mind, I would be most grateful if you could let me know whether or not there is anything of animal origin in Coca-Cola?

Yours faithfully
T Ravenscroft (Mr)

*

Coca-Cola Great Britain

Mr T Ravenscroft
17 Lingland Road
New Mills
Cheshire

Dear Mr Ravenscroft

Thank you for your letter of 28th April. I have only just received your letter today and so I must apologise for this delayed reply.

Your letter was originally received by Coca-Cola and Schweppes Beverages who then forwarded it on to myself. I hope that you will receive this reply before the arrival of your visitors as I am pleased to confirm that Coca-Cola does not contain any ingredients of animal origin. I hope that you and your family will continue to enjoy the refreshing taste of Coca-Cola and thank you for your interest in the products of The Coca-Cola Company.

Yours sincerely
T S Dean.

17 Lingland Road
New Mills
CHESHIRE

9th June

T S Dean
Coca-Cola Great Britain
1 Queen Caroline Street
London

Dear T S Dean

Thank you for your letter of 20th May. In fact my friends Arnold and Concepta are staying with us at the moment, so immediately I received your letter I offered them a Coca-Cola. Both of them however declined the offer and gave me a funny look. I then showed them your letter, but they still couldn't be tempted, and refused to say why. I then told them that they didn't know what they were missing. Arnold said he knew exactly what they were missing, which was why he was intent on missing it, and that they never drank Coca-Cola. When I asked him why he said it was because one of its ingredients is coca, a substance which is derived from the dried leaves of the coca plant, a South American shrub (Erythroxylon Coca), which is used to make the illegal drug cocaine. I told him not to be so silly as I'd once seen Michael Jackson promoting it on a television commercial, and that whilst Michael Jackson may well have been accused of anything from playing hide the sausage with young boys to trying to gradually turn himself into a white man he was definitely not the sort of person who would promote a beverage whose ingredients included an illegal substance.

However Arnold insisted that this is the case. Personally I think he's talking a load of hogwash - he's a social worker - but I must confess that I've often wondered why it is that a can of Coke can put me on a high whilst no other drink can do this.

Is it possible that Arnold could be telling the truth?

Yours faithfully

T Ravenscroft (Mr)

*

Coca-Cola Great Britain

2 July

Mr T Ravenscroft
17 Lingland Road
New Mills
Cheshire

Dear Mr Ravenscroft

Thank you for your letter of 9 June.

We can confirm that cocaine is not contained in Coca-Cola or in any other product of The Coca-Cola Company. The products of The Coca-Cola Company available in the United Kingdom are listed below.

Coca-Cola
Cherry Coke
diet Coke

caffeine-free diet Coke
Sprite
Sprite light
Lilt Pineapple and Grapefruit
diet Lilt Pineapple and Grapefruit
Lilt Mandarin and Mango
diet Lilt Mandarin and Mango
Fanta Orange
diet Fanta Orange
Five Alive Citrus
Five Alive Mediterranean
Five Alive Orchard Fruits
Five Alive Tropical
Five Alive Lite

With regard to your query on the coca plant, decocainized coca extract is a flavouring ingredient approved by the U.S. Food and Drug Administration under its exhaustive listing of natural ingredients "generally recognised as safe" and also by the Council of Europe, The Flavour Extract Manufacturers Association (FEMA) and the International Organisation of Flavour Industries (IOFI). If you have concerns about coca extract may I suggest that you contact one of the above organisations for further information. I hope this information is helpful to you and thank you for your interest in the products of the Coca-Cola Company.

Yours sincerely
T S Dean

*

17 Lingland Road
New Mills
CHESHIRE

4th July

T S Dean
Coca-Cola Great Britain
London

Dear T S Dean

Thank you for your letter of 2nd July. I showed it to my friend Arnold and he asked me to apologise to you on his behalf.

My elder son Marcus also saw your letter and expressed a great deal of interest in it. He will be leaving school this year and has intimated to me that he would like to work for the Coca-Cola Company. He even knows which job he would like to do - operating the apparatus which removes the cocaine from the coca extract. This is the first time he has ever shown any interest in work whatsoever, so naturally I am keen to encourage him. With this in mind perhaps you could send me a job application form for him?

Yours faithfully

T Ravenscroft (Mr)

*

Coca-Cola Great Britain

18 July

Mr T Ravenscroft
17 Lingland Road
New Mills
Cheshire

Dear Mr Ravenscroft

Thank you for your letter of 4 July.

There are very limited openings in the Company at the moment. However, your son is welcome to send a curriculum vitae to me and I shall give it to the staffing director in this office.

Once again thank you for your interest.

Yours sincerely

T S Dean

****

17 Lingland Road
New Mills
CHESHIRE

4th July
Ferrero Ltd
Rickmansworth
Herts

Dear Ferrero

On the recommendation of a friend I recently purchased a jar of your Nutella Hazlenut Chocolate Spread. It was quite tasty, but despite going through it with a fine toothcomb I could find no trace of any hazelnuts whatsoever. Is it possible I got a faulty jar?

Yours faithfully

T Ravenscroft (Mr)

*

FERRERO

15 April
Mr T Ravenscroft
17 Lingland Road
New Mills
Cheshire

Dear Mr Ravenscroft
8

Thank you for your recent letter regarding hazelnuts in Nutella.

In the production process for Nutella there are rollers that grind the paste until it is smooth. That is why you cannot feel the nuts.

Thank you for writing and I now enclose a jar which I hope you will enjoy.

Yours sincerely

Karen Davies
Customer Relations Department

*

17 Lingland Road
New Mills
CHESHIRE

18th April

Karen Davies
Ferrero UK Ltd
Rickmansworth
Herts

Dear Karen Davies

Thank you for your letter of 15th April and the free jar of Nutella. Yes, I am sure I will enjoy it - the quality of Nutella was never in any doubt, it was just that as your label said 'Hazelnut Chocolate Spread' I not unreasonably expected something with nuts in it. Maybe you should consider making your label a little clearer in this regard?

Now I have some good news for you! I believe you may have accidentally stumbled on a really exciting new advertising slogan for your product. It is contained in the last sentence of your letter. I refer of course to your phrase 'You cannot feel the nuts!' (The exclamation mark is mine.) It definitely has a ring to it, that certain *je ne sais quoi* which all great advertising slogans have, a sort of cross between 'You can't tell Stork from butter' and 'Nuts, whole hazelnuts, Cadburys make 'em and they cover them with chocolate'. If you were to use this slogan in a TV commercial I am quite sure the sales of Nutella would hit the roof. Comedy is used to great effect in commercials these days, so might I suggest the following:-

SCENE: A SULTAN'S HAREM.

A EUNUCH IS SPOONING NUTELLA INTO HIS MOUTH DIRECTLY FROM THE JAR, WITH OBVIOUS ENJOYMENT. ONE OF THE SULTAN'S WIVES, SCANTILY-DRESSED IN BRA AND DIAPHANOUS PANTALOONS, IS FONDLING THE EUNUCH IN THE GROIN AREA OF HIS TROUSERS. THEY TURN TO THE CAMERA IN UNISON AND SAY: -

"You cannot feel the nuts!"

Or is that a bit too saucy? I look forward to hearing from you with your comments.

Yours faithfully

T Ravenscroft (Mr)

*

FERRERO

Mr T Ravenscroft
17 Lingland Road
New Mills
Cheshire

Dear Mr Ravenscroft

Thank you for your second letter regarding Nutella.

I will pass your suggestion for the new Nutella advertisement on to my colleagues in the Marketing Department.

Once again, thank you for taking the time and trouble to write.

Yours sincerely

Karen Davies
Customer Relations Department

****

17 Lingland Road
New Mills
CHESHIRE

18th March

Ena Baxter
Baxters of Speyside Ltd
Fochabers
Moray
Scotland

Dear Baxter's Soup

I have been buying your Cock-a-Leekie soup for many years, and an absolutely splendid soup it is too. It is with no small regret then that I must now make a complaint about it; for on opening my most recent can, taste buds at the ready and appetite fully whetted, I was surprised to discover that the contents of the can were ninety per cent rice. Now I like rice as much as the next man - as long as the next man isn't a Chinaman of course - but ninety per cent is a bit too much rice even for a man who likes rice.

There is no doubt a fault with your rice dispenser and you would do well to have it checked out. Fortunately I had another can of Cock-a-Leekie in the cupboard, and I am happy to report that on opening it I found it to be well up to Baxters' usual excellent standard.

I am sure that being Scottish you will be glad to learn that the original faulty can wasn't wasted. Parsimony as well as necessity being the mother of invention, I drained off what little liquid there was, added milk and sugar to taste, and had it as a rice pudding for afters. And very nice it was too, the slight chicken flavour of the rice adding more than a little extra interest to what can sometimes be a rather dull pudding. In fact, thinking about it, if you ever feel the urge to add puddings to your catalogue of culinary goodies you could do a lot worse than market it yourselves. Maybe you could call it 'Cock-of-Puddings'?

Yours faithfully

T Ravenscroft (Mr)

*

BAXTERS

24 March
Reference : 20517
Mr Ravenscroft
17 Lingland Road
New Mills
Cheshire

Dear Mr Ravenscroft

Thank you for your letter of 18 March, to which Mrs Ena Baxter has asked me to give my immediate, personal attention. May I first of all say how concerned we are at Baxters to learn of your disappointment with the can of our Cock-a-Leekie Soup which you purchased recently.

We are always pleased to hear from customers how much they enjoy our products and therefore we are consequently all the
13

more concerned that you have purchased one which does not come up to the high standard you have come to expect.

We make our soup in huge kettles, much larger than the original Mrs Baxter ever used, and although the mix is heated up to boiling point, the vegetables are not actually "cooked" until they are sealed in a can. We do notice that, even with the huge stirrers we use, the bottom of the kettle can be thicker than the top. As we are aware of this, we take the first and the last few cans off to ensure that our discerning consumers only have the traditional Cock-a- Leekie Soup normally associated with Baxters. It would appear in this instance that you have purchased one of the cans which should have been removed. You may be sure, however, that your complaint will be the subject of investigation with our Production Manager. In order to assist us with our investigation I would be grateful if you could return to us the coded end of the can concerned, if this is still available; unfortunately the bar code on the label does not give us the information we require. I enclose a prepaid envelope for this purpose.

As a gesture of our goodwill, I have pleasure in enclosing some vouchers which will enable you to obtain replacement Baxter products from your local store. I hope you will accept these with our compliments and that you enjoy the products you choose. Also enclosed is some information about our Visitors Centre which I hope you will find of interest.

Assuring you of our best attention at all times.

Yours sincerely,

Miss M Macpherson
Quality Audit Manager

*

17 Lingland Road
New Mills
CHESHIRE

1st April

Miss M Macpherson
Baxters of Speyside Ltd
Fochabers

Your ref 20517

Dear Miss Macpherson

Thank you for your prompt and informative reply, and for the gift vouchers, which I passed on to the needy. However, your letter leaves me confused to say the least. You write that you make your soup in huge kettles, 'much larger than the original Mrs. Baxter ever used', yet your television advertisement clearly shows Edna Baxter making the soup in her kitchen using ordinary utensils. Perhaps you can clear this up for me?

I look forward to your reply.

Yours faithfully

T Ravenscroft (Mr)

PS. Since my initial letter to you I have become a real fan of Cock-a-Leekie flavoured rice pudding. If you'd like to try it for yourself I've found that 85 per cent Ambrosia Creamed Rice to 15 per cent Cock-a-Leekie Soup gives the best results. If you were to market this as Cock-of-Puddings I am quite sure you would have a winner on your hands.

*

BAXTERS

Mr Ravenscroft
17 Lingland Road
New Mills
Cheshire

Dear Mr Ravenscroft

Thank you for your letter of 1st April, further to your complaint about a can of our Cock-a-Leekie Soup.

The television advert depicting Mrs Baxter shows her developing new recipes in her kitchen. These recipes are then transferred into the factory where we indeed use huge kettles in the preparation of over 50 million cans of soup per year.

I hope this satisfactorily answers your enquiry and that we can continue to count on your valued custom.
Assuring you of our best attention at all times.

Yours sincerely,

Miss M Macpherson
Quality Audit Manager

*

17 Lingland Road
New Mills
CHESHIRE

11th April

Your ref 20517
Miss M Macpherson
Quality Audit Manager
Baxters of Speyside
Fochabers

Dear Miss Macpherson

You can always count on my valued custom. I have been enjoying your soups ever since I can remember, and the fact that you choose to mislead the general public with your television commercial won't stop me now.

You didn't mention whether or not you might have any interest in my idea for 'Cock-of Puddings'. Since I last wrote to you I have improved it with the addition of a little nutmeg and a hint of honey, and it really is quite something now, even if I say so myself. I had friends round for dinner the other evening and served it up as desert with a spoonful of Robertson's Raspberry Jam, and everyone present voted it an unqualified success. Indeed Laura Barker remarked that it was 'to die for'.

My kindest regards to you.

Yours faithfully

T Ravenscroft (Mr)

*

BAXTERS

22 April
Reference : 20517
Mr Ravenscroft
17 Lingland Road
New Mills
Cheshire

Dear Mr Ravenscroft

Thank you very much for your recent letter, further to your original complaint about a can of our Cock-a-Leekie Soup.

We do not make desserts and hence my not picking up on your 'Cock of Pudding' suggestion.

Assuring you of our best attention at all times.

Yours sincerely,

Miss M Macpherson
Quality Audit Manager

*

17 Lingland Road
New Mills
CHESHIRE

25th April

Your ref 20517

Dear Miss Macpherson

I was sorry to learn that you don't make desserts, but then at one time you didn't make soups did you, so I'm quite sure you will change your mind once you've tasted Cock-of- Puddings, a sample of which I enclose. And here's a snap of it that you may like to use in your advertising campaign for it, which I feel sure you are bound to mount.

This is the definitive version, and consists of four parts of Ambrosia Creamed Rice to one part of Baxters Cock-a-Leekie

19

Soup, half a teaspoon of honey, quarter of a teaspoon of minced root ginger, and a little nutmeg. Utter bliss!

I haven't got canning facilities of course, but the old salmon tin I have put it in has been thoroughly sterilised in Milton, before re-sealing the tin lid with superglue, so you have nothing to fear on the health front.

My family and I plan to visit your Visitor Centre on the 23rd of May, and your factory the following day, all being well. By then you and Ena Baxter will have had the chance to sample Cock-of-Puddings and evaluate it. Indeed I will be very surprised if you're not producing it in vast quantities in one of your huge kettles by then. Whereabouts is you office, I'll drop in on you?

Incidentally, the expression 'to die for', which I told you was used by Laura Barker to describe Cock-of-Pudding, proved to be a little unfortunate, as two days later she dropped dead. But I'm quite sure it had nothing to do with the pudding.

My regards to you.

Yours faithfully

T Ravenscroft (Mr)

*

BAXTERS

9 May
Reference : 20517
Mr Ravenscroft
17 Lingland Road
New Mills
Cheshire

Dear Mr Ravenscroft

Thank you for your most recent letter about your Cock of Puddings. Unfortunately the sample which you kindly returned to us had deteriorated in the post therefore I am sure you would appreciate our reluctance to taste it.

Finally, I do hope you enjoy your visit to the factory in May. Unfortunately I will be away on holiday in the USA that week, but I am sure that the Visitor Centre staff will ensure your visit is most enjoyable.

Yours sincerely,

Miss M Macpherson
Quality Audit Manager

*

17 Lingland Road
New Mills
CHESHIRE

11th May
Your ref 20517
Miss M Macpherson
Quality Audit Manager
Baxter's of Speyside Ltd
Fochabers

Dear Miss Macpherson

Coward!

Yours faithfully

T Ravenscroft (Mr)

****

Spam
Thetford
Norfolk

Dear Spam

About a month ago I at last took the plunge, bought myself a computer, and became a Silver Surfer (actually I am a bald surfer but I believe Silver Surfer is the name that has been conferred upon old age pensioner computer owners).

With the computer and internet connection came email, which I find very handy. One thing I don't find very handy is all the unsolicited email I am now receiving. Up to fifty messages a day and increasing daily. A younger friend who has been surfing for some time and has experience in these matters tells me that this unwanted mail is called Spam.

Which is the reason I am writing to you. Just what is your game? I can't for the life of me think why you should want to do this, except to make money. Why can't you people at Spam be satisfied doing what you are good at, i.e. making excellent chopped pork and ham luncheon meat, and stop sending people messages they don't want? The other day I had one asking me if I wanted to buy an inflatable rubber woman! Not only was this disgusting but at £11.90 it was very poor value too.

Kindly remove my name of your mailing list at once.

T Ravenscroft (Mr)

SPAM up for the taste

Mr T Ravenscroft
17 Lingland Road
New Mills
CHESHIRE

Dear Mr Ravenscroft

Thank you for your letter of 31 March regarding Spam. We would like to assure you that we are not responsible for the SPAM mail you have been receiving during your email.

Spam mail is defined by the University of Glasgow as:-

"unsolicited, or 'junk' email that is analogous to unwanted circulars that are received in paper mail."

and is in no way linked with our company. If you wish to prevent unsolicited emails there are many different methods available on the internet to prevent such mail that can be found via an internet search.

Whilst you are on the internet you may wish to visit our site at www.spam-uk.com where you are sure to find lots of real SPAM information, comments and recipes.

I hope this information is of use to you and would like to thank you for your interest in our brand.

Yours Sincerely

Stuart Neal
Technical Assistant.

17 Lingland Road
New Mills
CHESHIRE

14th April

Stuart Neil
Spam
Thetford

Dear Stuart Neal

Ref your reply to my letter of 31 March.

Do I feel a fool! Thanks for putting me right. Thanks also for pointing me in the direction of your very interesting and informative website, on which I spent a pleasant half-hour or so this morning (after I had got rid of yesterday's Spam). I shall certainly be trying your Stinky French Garlic Spam, which sounds like heaven to a garlic lover like me.

In fact your informing me of your website has solved a little problem I had vis-à-vis my other half. Her birthday is coming up very shortly and as usual I didn't know what to get her. I do now. A pair of your Spam Earrings, price £9.50. I have sent for a pair and can't wait to see her face when I give them to her.

T Ravenscroft (Mr)

*

17 Lingland Road
New Mills
CHESHIRE

Stuart Neil
Technical Assistant
Spam
Thetford

Dear Stuart Neal

Further to my letter of 14th April. The Spam earrings arrived just in time for my wife's birthday, and very nice they were too. She said that she liked them as much as she likes Spam, which is quite a lot, but thanks all the same but she didn't want them as she has several friends who are vegetarians and if she were to wear the Spam earrings in their company it wouldn't be in very good taste. I was therefore left with a pair of Spam earrings on my hands. However, so that they wouldn't be a complete waste of money I decided to open them and have the Spam on a sandwich. Imagine my surprise when on opening up the little tins I found them to be more or less solid metal with not a trace of Spam inside!

This is quite beyond the pale. I realise they are only earrings but they are Spam earrings and as such should contain Spam in them. And now they can't even be used as earrings as I ruined them beyond repair trying to get the non-existent Spam out. I would be interested in your observations and my money back.

Yours sincerely

T Ravenscroft (Mr)

NO REPLY!

17 Lingland Road
New Mills
CHESHIRE

19th March

McVities
Admail 827
Fakenham
Norfolk

Dear McVities

I'm afraid that I have a rather serious complaint to make about
one of your vegetarian products. I'm a vegetarian and yesterday I
purchased a packet of your Linda McCartney Deep Country Pies
from my local supermarket, and later heated them up for supper
along with some oven chips, for my three children and myself. I
have to report that in at least one of the pies, the pie eaten by me,
was a quantity of meat. It is difficult to believe that with a pie
whose ingredients already include water, wheatflour, vegetable
oil, onion, rehydrated soya protein concentrate, vegetarian
seasoning, modified starch, wheat protein, soya flour, salt, malt
extract and sodium, that there would be any room left in it for
meat, but meat in it there was. There could very well have been
meat in the other three pies as well, but unfortunately my
children had eaten them before I had the chance to check. (The
speed with which my children dispatched the pies would suggest
that they did indeed contain meat, since they are reluctant
vegetarians at best, and anything put before them with meat in it
tends to go down their throats without touching the sides.)

Needless to say I am very disappointed in your 'vegetarian' pies and certainly won't be buying any more.

I would like your comments on this as I may decide to take the matter further with the appropriate authorities.

Yours faithfully

T Ravenscroft (Mr)

*

McVities

Our Ref: CW0064

8 April
Mr Ravenscroft
17 Lingland Road
New Mills
Cheshire

Dear Mr Ravenscroft

I write further to your letter dated the 1st April, regarding your complaint of a recent purchase of our Linda McCartney Deep Country Pies, which you believe contained meat. On behalf of the Company I would like to apologise for the upset and the inconvenience that you have been caused.

I would like to assure you that the products in our range are produced in a factory in Norfolk, which is totally dedicated to the Linda McCartney range and no other products are made there. The factory is totally meat free and the staff canteen is also totally vegetarian as no meat is allowed on site. This new factory took in a number of environmentally friendly issues during building, eg, uses ozone-friendly ammonia refrigerants, catalytic converters and natural gas.

A number of our products including the Deep Country Pies contain Textured Vegetable Protein which, not only looks like meat, but also has a similar taste. This is a meat substitute, ideal for Vegetarians, who, whilst liking the taste and texture of meat, are against the slaughter of animals.

The factory Technical Manager at the production unit concerned has assured me that controls within the factory are very strict: and the staff are fully aware on the handling of vegetarian products.

I hope I have allayed your fears, as all of our vegetarian customers are very important to us. We would have liked the opportunity to discuss this matter further with you over the telephone and are sorry that you feel you are unable to phone us, however if you would like someone to phone on your behalf we will gladly discuss this matter with them for you. It would also be useful to know if there is any remaining product available so that we can have it analysed to help put your mind at ease.

Once again I would like to thank you for the time and trouble you have taken to contact us about your complaint and I look forward to hearing from you, a stamped addressed envelope is enclosed for your convenience.

Assuring you of our best attention at all times.

Yours sincerely

Mrs Angie Wilding

Customer Care Department

*

17 Lingland Road
New Mills
CHESHIRE

10th April

Your ref CW0064

Angie Wilding
McVitie's Prepared Foods
Ross House
Grimsby

Dear Angie Wilding

Thank you for your very informative letter of 8th April. Having read it I feel that I could almost start up a vegetarian products factory myself! You are to be congratulated on making textured vegetable protein both resemble and taste like meat. It would fool Desperate Dan himself. It certainly fooled me!

On reflection I think I may have been guilty of pre-judging your Linda McCartney Deep Country Pies. Before I became a veggie I was convinced that most people benefited from a bit of meat inside them now and again, as my wife would concur, but I am now convinced that Linda's pies are a more than adequate substitute. They certainly must have benefited Paul McCartney – would he have been able to pen such a classic as 'The Frog Chorus' if he was still a meat eater? I doubt it very much.

Since my original letter I have tried some more of your range of Deep Country Pies, and I must say I was most impressed, as was my family. It is my hope to get my family completely vegetarian this year, including our pets, and your excellent range of products can only but help me to achieve this ambition. Our canary is already vegetarian of course, but our dog Rantzen still insists on bits of Chum mixed in with his dog biscuits. Are your Deep Country Pies fit for dogs? If so I could try mixing bits of them in instead.

I look forward to hearing from you.

Yours faithfully

T Ravenscroft (Mr)

*

McVities

Our Ref: CW0064
14 April
Mr Ravenscroft
17 Lingland Road
New Mills
Cheshire

Dear Mr Ravenscroft

I write further to your letter dated the 10th April regarding your complaint of a recent purchase of our Linda McCartney Deep Country Pies.

I would like to thank you for taking the time and trouble to write back to us regarding this matter and I am pleased that we have been able to restore your confidence in our vegetarian products.

For your information a vegetarian dog food called Best, produced by Oscar Pet Foods has been launched. This Company has nothing to do with McVities but they did work very closely with Linda McCartney. Should you wish to contact them, there address is:

Oscar Pet Foods
Bannister Hall Mill
Higher Walton
Preston
Lancs

Please find enclosed with our compliments the enclosed vouchers to the value of £5.00 as a gesture of our concern and goodwill to enable you to purchase products of your choice from our extensive range.

Yours sincerely

Mrs Angie Wilding
Customer Care Department

*

17 Lingland Road
New Mills
CHESHIRE

Angie Wilding
McVitie's Prepared Foods
Ross House
Grimsby

Dear Angie Wilding

I just thought I'd let you know that I took your advice and purchased some Best vegetarian dog food and tried it out on our dog Rantzen. I'm happy to report that the following day he bit the postman, so it would seem it is keeping him just as sharp as his usual Chum. Actually I tried a couple of spoonfuls of it myself and in taste found it to be quite indistinguishable from Linda McCartney Sausages, so I am not in the least surprised to learn that Linda worked closely with Oscar Pet Foods. Whether or not I will be able to put up with Rantzen eating vegetarian dog food is another matter, as it appears to have made him quite flatulent. I had a word about it with Oscar Pet Foods and they said that this was normal and that he would soon 'settle down'. I hope so, while we've still got some paint on the walls.

Actually since upping my intake of Linda McCartney products I've had a few problems in that area myself. Apart from trying to look innocent and pretending that it's somebody else, is there anything that can be done about this? Or, like Rantzen, will I soon settle down?

Yours faithfully

T Ravenscroft (Mr)

*

McVities

Our Ref: CW0064
30th April
Mr Ravenscroft
17 Lingland Road

New Mills
Cheshire

Dear Mr Ravenscroft

Thank you for your recent letter, I was very pleased to hear that you managed to find the Vegetarian Dog Food which we informed you about. It is known that people that are not used to soya and vegetable proteins in their diet, sometimes suffer with flatulence or similar symptoms at first but once the body gets used to the foods in the system this will settle down.

I would like to thank you once again for taking the time and trouble to write to us and I hope that you will continue to enjoy our range of Linda McCartney Foods.

Yours sincerely

Mrs Angie Wilding
Customer Care Department

****

17 Lingland Road
New Mills
CHESHIRE
20th March

CWS Ltd
MANCHESTER
M14 2YY
Dear CWS

The Co-op hasn't often given me cause to praise their products, your foodstuffs being more synonymous with convenience rather than Epicurean delights, but I must say that with your Co-op Egg Lasagne you are right up there with Marks and Spencers. Praise indeed, as I have something of a reputation as a lasagne buff. However, I can honestly say that your lasagne was the second most enjoyable that I have ever tasted, bested only by the truly mouth-watering lasagne served to the fortunate passengers of Air 2000, which is well worth the price of the flight alone. (I once tried to obtain the recipe from them but they wouldn't give it to me, so no fools them!)

Have you any other products in the same range? Even if they are only half as good as your lasagne I would be very keen to try them.

Yours faithfully
T Ravenscroft (Mr)

*

CWS

Our Ref: 195215
Mr Ravenscroft
17 Lingland Road
New Mills
Cheshire

Dear Mr Ravenscroft

Thank you for letting me know about your recent purchase of Co-op Egg Lasagne. We always make every effort to ensure our products meet the high standards that we specify and I am very sorry that on this occasion you have been disappointed. We do routinely check all our suppliers to ensure that the high standards we insist upon are being met and we shall be informing them of your complaint.

As a token of my regret I have enclosed gift vouchers to the value of £2.00 for any inconvenience incurred. If I can be of any further assistance, please do not hesitate to contact me.
Yours sincerely

Jean Jackson
Customer Relations

*

17 Lingland Road
New Mills
Cheshire
1st April

Your ref 195215
Jean Jackson
CWS
MANCHESTER

Dear Jean Jackson

Thank you for your letter of 25th March. Your reply really does beggar belief! I wrote to you in praise of one of your products and you replied with a letter of apology! This worries me more than somewhat, as it would indicate that you at the Co-op receive so many letters of complaint that regardless of its contents you rattle off an apology in reply to every letter you receive.

Please reassure me that this isn't the case, before my confidence in your company is destroyed forever. And you still haven't answered my original query, so I will repeat it. Have you any other products in the same range as your Co-op Egg Lasagne?

Yours faithfully

T Ravenscroft (Mr)

CWS

Our Ref: 195215
Mr Ravenscroft
17 Lingland Road
New Mills
Cheshire

Dear Mr Ravenscroft

Thank you for your letter regarding Co-op Egg Lasagne. Firstly may I apologise for the error in my original reply to you.

We are happy that you are pleased with this product and you may be sure that we will do everything possible to maintain the quality and value in accordance with your kind remarks.

The other products available in this range are as follows: Co-op Lasagne Verdi, Co-op Lasagne Co-op Tagliatelle and Co-op Vegetable Lasagne.

If you have any other comments, or I can be of any help in the future, please do not hesitate to contact me.

Yours sincerely

Jean Jackson, Customer Relations

*

17 Lingland Road
New Mills
Cheshire

7th April

Your ref 195215
Jean Jackson
CWS Ltd
Manchester

Dear Jean Jackson

Thank you for your letter. Since I last wrote to you something quite exciting has happened! As I mentioned to you in my original letter I am something of a lasagne nut, and when you have read the following words you will realise the reason for my excitement, as it seems I may have made something of a breakthrough in the fields of lasagne technology.

Last Friday I had to make one of my frequent flights to the Czech Republic on business. Now I don't know if you are at all familiar with the food served upon CSK Czechoslovak Airlines, but is not to be recommended (Incidentally, on no account let any of the cabin staff get anywhere near your false teeth). To avoid the airline's food I usually take a sandwich, but on this occasion the bread bin was empty so I had to think of something else. Now I don't know why, other than the fact that I am lasagne

39

mad, but I then had the brainwave of heating up one of your Co-op Egg Lasagnes and putting it in a thermos flask. It was a bit tricky spooning it in, and it did cause quite a few stares from my fellow passengers when I upended the flask and shook it out onto a plate, but the time and effort were well worth it. Whether it had something to do with the cabin pressure, or whether it was because it had spent some time in a thermos flask, I don't know; but what I do know without any shadow of doubt is that your lasagne from a flask at 30,000 feet is different class, indeed the equal to the lasagne of Air 2000! Believe me, it was like eating ambrosia. (The food of the Gods, that is, not the rice pudding, which can be quite nice, but somewhat inconsistent.)

Following the experience I tried out an experiment at home. First I heated up another of your lasagnes and spooned it into a thermos flask, left it for a few hours, then tried it. It was the equal of the lasagne I had on the aeroplane! I then enlisted the aid of a few neighbours and blind tested your lasagne heated up in the normal manner against your lasagne heated up then put into a thermos flask for several hours. Every one of the testers vastly preferred 'Egg Lasagne Thermos Flask'!

Bearing the above in mind I think that you should seriously consider recommending this method of preparing your lasagne on the packet. Or maybe you could alter your manufacturing process to include your lasagne resting in a giant thermos flask for a few hours before packaging? What do you think?

Yours faithfully

T Ravenscroft (Mr)

*

CWS

Our Ref: 195215
11.April
Mr Ravenscroft
17 Lingland Road
New Mills
Cheshire

Dear Mr Ravenscroft

Thank your letter regarding Co-op Vegetable Lasagne.

I have noted your comments but do not know if this idea would be practical, however I will be sure to pass on your suggestion to the appropriate department for interest or action as necessary.

We were pleased to hear that you enjoy this product and enclosed with our compliments is a Goodwill Voucher for £2.00 to enable you to try other Co-op products.

Yours sincerely

Jean Jackson
Customer Relations

*

17 Lingland Road
New Mills
Cheshire

16th April

Your ref 195215
Jean Jackson
CWS Ltd
MANCHESTER

Dear Jean Jackson

I am not at all happy that you do not feel able to bring about an undoubted improvement in your Co-op Vegetable Lasagne. I am not at all happy about the reckless abandon with which you appear to throw about Goodwill Vouchers for £2.00 either. No wonder the Co-op can't afford to pay divi out any more!

Yours faithfully

T Ravenscroft (Mr)

NO REPLY!

****

17 Lingland Road
New Mills
CHESHIRE

Butcher's Pet Care Ltd
Crick
Northants

Dear Sir

I am writing to congratulate you on a truly excellent product. I have just dined on a can of your Butcher's Tripe Mix, which I had with a portion of oven chips, and it was quite superb. With a bottle of Beaujolais to wash it down it felt almost like I was back in the Dordogne. At long last we have a British manufacturer has succeeded in doing with offal what the French have been doing with it for years. God bless you!

I do however have one minor criticism. Why do you refer to your tripe as an 'animal derivative' on the label? Tripe is offal, nothing more, nothing less, and to call it anything else is to pretend that it is something it isn't. There is nothing wrong with offal, believe me, I've eaten tons of it, and I shall be eating even more tons of it if you keep up the standard of your wonderful Butcher's Tripe Mix. A question though. Why is there a picture of a dog on the label?

Yours faithfully

T Ravenscroft (Mr)

*

BUTCHER'S PET CARE

11 April

Mr Ravenscroft
17 Lingland Road
New Mills
Cheshire

Dear Mr Ravenscroft

Thank you for your letter congratulating us on our Butcher's Tripe Mix product.

We receive many similar letters from satisfied owners writing to us on behalf of their dog. Yours is the first letter we have had from a human consumer. The Feeding Stuffs Regulations 1995 require us by law to describe tripe on the label under the heading meat and animal derivatives. The term offal is not permitted although as you point out it is nothing to be ashamed of.

Please remember Butcher's Tripe Mix is a complementary food and to keep your nose wet and coat in tip top condition you must eat it mixed with an equal quantity of reputable mixer meal. Please find enclosed £5 worth of vouchers towards your future purchases.

Yours sincerely

Ian Cresswell
Technical Manager

*

17 Lingland Road
New Mills
CHESHIRE

Ian Cresswell
Butcher's Ltd
Crick

Dear Ian Cresswell

Thank you for your letter of 24th April, and the vouchers, which I passed on to the needy. It would appear that I have made a mistake and that Butcher's Tripe Mix is a dog food! Perhaps it is understandable though, I mean on boxes of Kellogg's Frosties there's a picture of a tiger but it would be a fool who claimed that tigers eat cornflakes, as I am sure you will agree.

Getting back to the point, your letter arrived too late to have any influence on a meal which I recently put on chez Ravenscroft for a potential client. However I doubt that it would have made any difference to the menu I had decided on, even if it had arrived before my client. In the event he said that the Tripes Provencal, made with your Butcher's Tripe Mix as the basis, was quite superb, and he couldn't believe that most of it had come out of a can. In fact when I showed him the can to prove it he was quite speechless. If I don't get a big order out of him I will be very surprised, although up to now he has been out of the office every time I've tried to contact him. I must say that I enjoyed your little joke about keeping my nose wet and my coat in tip top

45

condition. Very funny!

Yours faithfully

T Ravenscroft (Mr)

****

17 Lingland Road

New Mills

CHESHIRE

4th April

The Jacob's Bakery Ltd

P.O.Box 1

Long Lane

Liverpool

Dear Jacob's Bakery

I am writing to you in my official capacity as secretary of the New Mills Invalids Club. This year marks the 25th anniversary of the club, and we mean to celebrate the occasion in some style, whilst at the same time giving club funds a much needed boost. To achieve this we intend to manufacture and sell to the general public a chocolate biscuit. We are confident that we have the expertise to accomplish this as four of our members used to work for the local sweet and confectionery factory - in fact it was because they worked at the local sweet and confectionery factory that they became invalids, having caught various parts of their anatomy in the machinery, but that's another matter.

Here is where you come in. I have long been a fan of your Jacob's Club biscuits, as have many of my fellow members, and to this end we would like to 'cash in' on your esteemed name by calling our biscuit a 'Jacob's Club Foot' biscuit. This would at once inform the public that it is a quality product, and also that it supports invalids. Can I have you permission, please?

Yours faithfully
T Ravenscroft (Mr)

*

JACOB'S

17th April
Mr Ravenscroft
Secretary: New Mills Invalids Club.
17 Lingland Road
New Mills
Cheshire

Dear Sir,

Thank you for your letter of 4th April requesting consent to bring out a chocolate covered biscuit called 'Club Foot' in connection with your society's forthcoming anniversary.

We have no objections to the proposals in your letter and hope it proves to a successful fund raiser. Our agreement is given on the understanding that you restrict sales to local fundraising events for a limited period and no mention of The Jacob's Bakery Limited is made on the packaging etc.

Yours sincerely

Gary Brookes
Legal and Finance Department

*

17 Lingland Road
New Mills
CHESHIRE

Gary Brookes
Legal & Finance Dept
The Jacob's Bakery Ltd
P.O.Box 1
Liverpool

Dear Gary Brookes

Thank you for your letter of 17th April.

The New Mills Invalids Club will be forever in your debt. I take note of your request that we do not mention The Jacob's Bakery Limited on our package. In fact I have gone one better, and have made absolutely sure that people will be under no illusions that our biscuits have anything to do with The Jacob's Bakery, as you will see from a perusal of a facsimile of our wrapper, below. It was designed by our Mr Hargreaves, who has one arm and an NVQ in graphic design, and I am sure you will agree he has made an excellent job of it.

Yours faithfully

T Ravenscroft (Mr)

*

JACOB'S

9th May
Mr Ravenscroft
17 Lingland Road
New Mills
Cheshire

Dear Sir,

Thank you for your letter of 28th April. As mentioned previously in my letter of 17th April, I would prefer it if no mention was made of The Jacob's Bakery Limited on the packaging.

Therefore, please could you remove from the packaging the statement 'Definitely nothing to do with The Jacob's Bakery Limited'.

Yours sincerely

Gary Brookes
Legal & Finance Dept
49

*

17 Lingland Road
New Mills
CHESHIRE

Gary Brookes
Legal & Finance Dept
The Jacob's Bakery Ltd
P.O.Box 1
Liverpool

Dear Gary Brookes

Thank you for your letter of 20th April. Unfortunately it arrived too late for me to alter the wording on our 'Club Foot' wrapper, so we went ahead with it as it was. Our anniversary was last Saturday and I am happy to report that it was an unqualified success, especially chocolate biscuit-wise. We made a total of 5000 biscuits and each and every one was sold. Not only that, the biscuits were enjoyed by all who bought them; in fact one man went so far as to say that our Club Foot biscuit was better than your Club biscuit, but I think he was just being nice to us, and anyway he isn't long out of the mental hospital and there are some who hold that he should never have been discharged.

I can report that the occasion was such a great success that we hope to make it an annual event. In closing, I and my fellow members would like to thank you from the bottom of our hearts. (Except for Mr Beasley, who has recently had a heart transplant, so he would like to thank you from the bottom of somebody else's heart)

Yours faithfully
T Ravenscroft (Mr)

*

JACOB'S

9th June

Mr Ravenscroft
Secretary: New Mills Invalids Club.
17 Lingland Road
New Mills
Cheshire

Dear Sir,

Thank you for your letter of 12th May. I am glad that your product proved to be such a great success and I hope it raised a substantial amount of money for your society.

It is a shame that we did not receive a sample of your product to show to our R & D department! May I take this opportunity to wish you every success with your future fund-raising events.

Yours sincerely

Gary Brookes
Legal & Finance Dept

****

17 Lingland Road
New Mills
CHESHIRE

5th April

Kentucky Fried Chicken
Pepsico Restaurants International
32 Goldsworth Road
Woking

Dear Kentucky Fried Chicken

I am a mature student taking an Open University degree course in Food Technology. At the moment I am gathering data for my thesis, which will be entitled 'Chicken, its Use and Abuse'. I have yet to decide whether or not coating a chicken in a secret recipe before plunging it into hot oil qualifies it as 'Abuse' but as Kentucky Fried Chicken is universally popular I will probably include it in the 'Use' section of the thesis.

I would be grateful for your help, and what I would like to know from you is this:- does the term Kentucky Fried Chicken mean (a) that you obtain your chickens from Kentucky and then fry them, (b) that the chickens can come from anywhere but are fried in Kentucky, or (c) that there is a breed of chicken called Kentucky Chicken. Or is it perhaps a mixture of all three?

Yours faithfully

T Ravenscroft (Mr)

*

PEPSICO EUROPE

Mr T Ravenscroft
17 Lingland Road
New Mills
Cheshire

Dear Mr Ravenscroft

In reply to your letter dated 10 April. Please find enclosed a pamphlet detailing the history of KFC.

Colonel Sanders who began KFC was from Kentucky and so he called the product Kentucky Fried Chicken. The chicken used is sourced in the country of origin, i.e. if you buy KFC in England the raw product comes from the UK. Once again, thanks for the interest you have shown in our brand.

Yours sincerely

Kerry Pinker
Customer Services

*

17 Lingland Road
New Mills
CHESHIRE
20th April

Your ref CC-00772-AS

Kerry Pinker
Pepsico Europe
Woking

Dear Kerry Pinker

Thank you for your letter and the informative pamphlet, which should be most useful.

It was with no little surprise that I learned the chickens used by your company are just ordinary chickens from the country of origin. This is because since writing to you events have conspired which absolutely convinced me that they must be some special breed of chicken. Allow me to explain. As part of the research for my thesis I stood outside a Kentucky Fried Chicken outlet for a complete day, questioning your customers as they came out. (I didn't question why they went in!) One of the things I was trying to establish was what exactly a 'piece' of Kentucky Fried Chicken is. On collating the answers of over two hundred customers it transpired that a 'piece' is a portion of a chicken from the leg, thigh or breast of the bird, but more usually from the leg or thigh - indeed if the proportions of breast to leg and thigh pieces used by the outlet in my research was representative of your other outlets then you must be using chickens which have one breast and thirty six legs – or in other words a special breed of chicken. However you now inform me that this is not the case. It just goes to prove the old saying 'There are lies, damned lies and statistics'.

Thank you for your help. I don't suppose there's any chance of getting hold of a copy of Colonel Sanders' secret recipe, is there?

Yours faithfully
T Ravenscroft (Mr)

NO REPLY!

****

17 Lingland Road
New Mills
CHESHIRE
24th March

Tesco Stores Ltd
Cheshunt

Dear Tesco

I have just finished a carton of your Healthy Eating Crème Fraiche D'isigny, and very nice it was too. In fact it was almost up to the standard of your regular Crème Fraiche D' Isigny, which I normally buy. Which brings me to the question: If your Healthy Eating Crème Fraiche D'Isigny is 'healthy eating' then, by definition, is your regular Crème Fraiche D'Isigny 'unhealthy eating'?

This is of no small concern to me because all things being equal I prefer your regular Crème Fraiche D'isigny - try dipping oven chips in it, absolutely gorgeous - but not at the expense of my health.

Looking forward to hearing from you.

Yours faithfully

T Ravenscroft (Mr)

*

TESCO

Our Ref: 453269
3 April
Mr T Ravenscroft
17 Lingland Road
New Mills
CHESHIRE

Dear Mr Ravenscroft

Thank you for your letter dated 24 March.

We are currently investigating this matter and will be contacting you again in the near future.

Thank you for taking the time to contact us.

Yours sincerely

For and on behalf of Tesco Stores Ltd

Glenn Pattison
Customer Services

*

17 Lingland Road
New Mills
CHESHIRE

23rd April

Your ref 453269

Glenn Pattison
Tesco
PO Box 73
Dundee

Dear Glenn Pattison

It is now over three weeks since you wrote to me. How are your investigations coming along? I must say that you are dragging your heels somewhat on this one, the Co-op were much quicker off the mark when I wrote to them about their lasagne. *And* they sent me a voucher.

Yours faithfully

T Ravenscroft (Mr)

*

TESCO

Our Ref: 453269
Mr T Ravenscroft
17 Lingland Road
New Mills
CHESHIRE

Dear Mr Ravenscroft

Thank you for your letter dated 24 March regarding Healthy Eating Creme Fraiche and please let me apologise for the delay in responding. With regards your query, I contacted our technologist who explained that the Healthy Eating range is designed around a number of things: For example, most are half the fat, lower in sodium salt or lower in sugar than the normal products. Thus they are aimed at customers who want to reduce their intake of certain substances. This is not to say that the normal products are 'unhealthy' just that our Healthy Eating products are a healthier option.

I hope this goes some way to answering your question and allays your fears about our non-Healthy Eating products. I hope you continue to enjoy our Creme Fraiche (with oven chips – may have to try that one!) Should you have any further queries do not hesitate to contact me.

Thank you for taking the time and trouble to write to us.

Yours sincerely

For and on behalf of Tesco Stores Ltd

Marc Turnbull
Customer Services Manager

*

17 Lingland Road
New Mills
CHESHIRE

Your ref 453269
Marc Turnbull
Tesco
PO Box 73

Dear Marc Turnbull

Thank you for your letter of 29th April.

I would suggest to you that your technologist is wasting his time at Tesco, for a successful career in politics as a spin doctor surely awaits him. If you are taking out quantities of fat, salt and sugar in order to make a product healthy then it follows that fat, salt and sugar are bad for our health; therefore his sentence 'This is not to say that the normal products are unhealthy, just that Healthy Eating products are a healthier option' is not only double-speak, but one of the finest examples of double-speak I have seen for ages, and worthy of Tony Blair himself. In truth it would make more sense to call your two varieties of crème fraiche 'Unhealthy Eating' and' Very Unhealthy Eating', but when was the last time a supermarket chain let the truth get in the way of a sale?

Yours faithfully

T Ravenscroft (Mr)

*

TESCO

Our Ref: 453269

Mr T Ravenscroft
17 Lingland Road
New Mills

Dear Mr Ravenscroft

Thank you for your letter dated 1 May.

As far as our technologist is concerned I'm sure he did in fact used to write in fact rite Tony Blair's speeches!!

I think that the wording 'Healthy Eating' is a little misleading as all food is healthy as it provides essential fuel for our bodies, to keep us going throughout the day. We all need certain amounts of fat, sugar, salt etc. to keep us fit and healthy. Obviously different foods contain differing amounts of each. So, this dispels the fact theory that non-healthy eating products are by definition unhealthy.

The healthy eating label helps to provide people with a choice and serves to make their shopping trips easier. For example, people who suffer from high cholesterol, heart disease, or diabetes, may wish to reduce their intake of fat, sugar or salt. By highlighting our products which have reduced levels of these this makes their shopping and perhaps their lives easier.

Conversely, what may be a healthy diet for a person suffering one of the above mentioned problems may not be suitable for someone else. This has been highlighted in the news recently, where some parents have been feeding their children low fat diets which are unsuitable for a child's health and growth. Hence it has resulted in children who are malnourished or who have stunted growth. So, in this case the so-called normal products would have been the healthy option.

With regard to your closing comment we are not totally sale oriented and, has been illustrated, more customer focused by endeavouring to meet our customers' needs, we are not lying to make a quick sale!

I hope this clears this up a little better. Thank you for taking the time and trouble to write to us.

Yours sincerely

For and on behalf of Tesco Stores Ltd

Marc Turnbull

Customer Services Manager

*

17 Lingland Road
New Mills
CHESHIRE

12th May

Marc Turnbull
Tesco
PO Box 73
Dundee

Dear Marc Turnbull

Well you've certainly put me in my place, and no mistake! Not to say enlightened me. Particularly so with regard to children's' low fat diets that are unsuitable for children's growth. This probably explains why my wife and myself, each brought up on roast and three veg, are both six footers, whilst our three children are of below average height. In fact our eldest, fifteen -year- old Marcus, is only four feet three. I can see now that I shall have to get them all off Heinz Weight Watcher Soups and Ambrosia Low Fat Rice Pudding and get them on to Big Macs and Syrup Pudding, before I do any permanent damage to them!

Thank you for your valuable advice. When I return from holiday next week I shall be writing a strong letter to Heinz and Ambrosia telling me that you have informed me that their Weight Watcher Soup and Low Fat Rice Pudding products are unhealthy for children, and that they should point this out on their Labels.

Yours faithfully

T Ravenscroft (Mr)

****

17 Lingland Road
New Mills
CHESHIRE

27th March

McCain Foods (GB) Ltd
Scarborough
North Yorkshire

Dear McCain Foods

I feel that the time is long overdue when I should write to you in praise of your McCain's Oven Chips. I honestly don't know what I would do without them. Well I do, but as it involves the mind-numbing task of peeling potatoes I would rather not think about it. The fact is that your oven chips are quite the best chips it has ever been my pleasure to eat, and as a Northerner know my chips. However I can't say that I think much of your cooking instructions, so rather than cook them in the oven or under the grill as you suggest, which tends to make them rather dry, I cook them in the good old fashioned way in a chip pan. This has the effect of making them much more succulent, believe me, especially when using good beef dripping as the frying medium.

The only thing that worries me about doing this is that there may be a possibility that the chip pan method of cooking oven chips uses more fat. Have my worries any foundation in fact or am I being over-cautious?

Yours faithfully

T Ravenscroft (Mr)

*

McCain

AC/SY 4 April
Mr T Ravenscroft
17 Lingland Road
New Mills
CHESHIRE

Dear Mr Ravenscroft

Thank you for your letter letting us know how you cook McCain Oven Chips.

As our Oven chips are fried in Sunflower Oil, and then you are frying them in dripping, you are nearly doubling the amount of fat on the chips. If you wish to fry your chips, me we recommend that you try some of our fry chips and we have enclosed a £1.00 McCain voucher to enable you to do so.

Yours sincerely

Ann Charlton (Mrs)
CONSUMER SERVICES MANAGER

Enc

*

17 Lingland Road
New Mills
CHESHIRE

9th April

Your ref AC/SY

Ann Charlton
Consumer Services Manager
McCain Foods (GB) Ltd
Scarborough

Dear Ann Charlton

Thank you for your letter of 4th April and the voucher.

I tried some of your fry chips but quite frankly found them to be a bit of a disappointment when compared with your oven chips. If I were you I would discontinue them and just sell oven chips, with something like 'Even Better Fried In Beef Dripping!' emblazoned on the packaging.

Incidentally, and with reference to the final sentence of your letter, when wishing to indicate that both yourself and your compatriots recommend something, it is only necessary to say 'we' and not 'me we', as you appear to think. Or is this an example of the Yorkshire dialect?

Yours faithfully

T Ravenscroft (Mr)

NO REPLY!

****

17 Lingland Road
New Mills
CHESHIRE
29th April

Kwik Save Stores Ltd
Warren Drive
Prestatyn

Dear Kwik Save

I have just had for lunch a can of your No Frills Baked Beans. Unfortunately, as well as having No Frills, the beans had No Taste either. Could it be possible, in an admittedly laudable attempt to force down prices, that by getting rid of the frills you have also got rid of the taste at the same time? I realise of course that No Frills is an 'own brand' product, and as such is probably made for you by one of the major food manufacturers and therefore somewhat out of your control, but it seems to me that they might be putting all the good beans into their own cans and sticking the inferior ones in your No Frills cans. If I were you I would have a word with them about it as they aren't doing your reputation any good at all. Do you happen to do a No Frills Lobster Bisque?

Yours faithfully

T Ravenscroft (Mr)

*

KWIK SAVE

Ref: 2999
9th May
Mr Ravenscroft
17 Lingland Road
New Mills
Cheshire

Dear Mr Ravenscroft

I was most concerned to learn of a complaint concerning a product purchased at one of our stores, and would like to offer my apologies on behalf of the Company.

To enable us to proceed with the investigation into this complaint, please return the product label and/or the foreign body using the packaging supplied, to this office at your earliest convenience. We take all complaints very seriously and a full investigation will commence as soon as we can forward the product/foreign body to the supplier. This may take several weeks as we will not only try to identify how the fault has arisen but also to help prevent a recurrence in the future.

We will be in touch with you again as soon as this process in complete, but should you like to contact us before then, please quote the above reference number. In the meantime, thank you for bringing this matter to our attention.

Yours sincerely

G H Williams (Mrs)
Customer Services Manager

*

17 Lingland Road
New Mills
CHESHIRE

15th May

G H Williams (Mrs)
Kwik Save Stores Ltd
Prestatyn

Dear Mrs Williams

I'm afraid I can't return the product to you as what I didn't eat I threw in the bin. However, since writing to you I have opened another can of your No Frills Baked Beans and can report that they were exactly the same as the others, i.e. poor, so this quality would appear to be the norm.

It seems to me that you have sent me a standard reply, since I made no reference in my letter to having found a foreign body in the beans. In fact I would have welcomed a foreign body in them as then they might have tasted of something.

I reiterate that my complaint is that your No Frills Baked Beans have No Taste. I also suggested that the reason for this might be that your manufacturers are using all the good beans for their own brand baked beans. I think it would serve your interests well if you challenged them on this. In the meantime what about my enquiry about No Frills Lobster Bisque?

Yours faithfully

T Ravenscroft (Mr)

*

KWIK SAVE

Ref: 2999
21st May
Mr Ravenscroft
17 Lingland Road
New Mills
Cheshire

Dear Mr Ravenscroft

I was most concerned to learn about a complaint concerning a product purchased at one of our stores, and would like to offer my apologies on behalf of the Company.

To enable us to proceed with the investigation into this complaint, please return the product label. This information is vital as we have more than one supplier and can not identify the can you have purchased. We take all complaints very seriously and a full investigation will commence as soon as we can identify the supplier forward on your comments. This may take several weeks as we will not only try to identify how the fault has arisen but also to help prevent a recurrence in the future.

We will be in touch with you again as soon as this process in complete, but should you like to contact us before then, please quote the above reference number. In the meantime, thank you for bringing this matter to our attention.

Yours sincerely

G H Williams (Mrs)
Customer Services Manager

*

17 Lingland Road
New Mills
CHESHIRE
27th May

G H Williams (Mrs)
Kwik Save Stores Ltd
Prestatyn

Dear Mrs Williams

Thank you for your letter of 21st May, which was a complete waste of time, as you only reiterated what you said in your letter of 9th May, which itself was a complete waste of time.

I suggest that you read both my previous letters carefully. Having done so you should realise that I do not have any of your No Frills Baked Beans left. And I most certainly won't be buying any more! Nor do I have the product label to return to you.

Is there any point in my asking, for the third time, if you do a No Frills Lobster Bisque? Or do you perhaps automatically ignore all enquiries as a matter of course?

Yours faithfully

T Ravenscroft (Mr)

*

KWIK SAVE

Our Ref: GHW/MW/2999
20th June
Mr Ravenscroft
17 Lingland Road
New Mills
Cheshire

Dear Mr Ravenscroft

We write further to our recent letters regarding your complaint with No Frills Baked Beans being tasteless.

We were extremely concerned to learn that you had found no taste to the beans, and would have liked to have informed the manufacturer so they could investigate further. Unfortunately, without codes from the packaging we are unable to identify which one of our four suppliers actually made the product.

However we can reassure you that the factories concerned have been thoroughly inspected for all aspects of manufacture and sampling checks are made on the product at regular intervals. We will nevertheless, keep details of your complaint on file should any other incidents of this nature arise.

Please accept our sincere apologies for this problem, and for disregarding your request for No Frills Lobster Bisque. This will be brought to the attention of the review committee who will consider this at the next range review meeting.

Thank you for bringing this matter to our attention, we appreciate the time and trouble you have taken to do this. We have pleasure in enclosing a £5.00 Kwik Save voucher to enable you to purchase replacement products, and hope that Kwik Save can continue to rely on your valued custom.

Yours sincerely

G H Williams (Mrs)
Customer Services Manager

*

17 Lingland Road
New Mills
CHESHIRE

23rd June

Your ref GHW/MW/2999

G H Williams (Mrs)

Kwik Save Stores Ltd
Prestatyn

Dear Mrs Williams

Thank you for the concern and the voucher, which I will keep until such time as you have introduced No Frills Lobster Bisque, which I feel quite sure you will be bringing out following your range revue meeting.

I would also urge you to consider adding No Frills Pate de Foie Gras avec Truffles to your list, as I am sure this would be a winner with gourmets on a limited income, as would a budget Chateau Petrus claret. Regarding the No Frills Lobster Bisque, might I suggest that you approach Baxter's of Speyside to manufacture it for you as their Lobster Bisque is excellent. You can mention that I recommended them to you if you like - they know me quite well from my creation Cock of Puddings, which I expect them to be adding to their list of foodstuffs soon.

Yours faithfully

T Ravenscroft (Mr)

*

KWIK SAVE

Our Ref: GHW/MW/2999
2nd July
Mr Ravenscroft
17 Lingland Road
New Mills
Cheshire

Dear Mr Ravenscroft

No Frills Pate De Foie Gras And Chateau Petrus Claret

Thank you for your recent letter regarding the possibility of stocking the above products in Kwik Save stores.

Kwik Save's aim is to provide loyal customers with the best value shopping basket anywhere. As we trade from units which are usually smaller than most of our competitors, we must pay constant attention not only to market trends but also to our customers when assessing store ranges. We carry out reviews at regular intervals and your suggestion will be considered at our next review meeting.

We do appreciate our customer's taking the time to make constructive suggestions which will improve the range of products and services we offer. Please do not hesitate to advise us of any other product you feel would be a worthwhile addition to our range.

Yours sincerely
G H Williams (Mrs)

*

17 Lingland Road
New Mills
CHESHIRE

3rd July

Your ref GHW/MW/2999
G H Williams (Mrs)
Kwik Save Stores Ltd
Prestatyn

Dear Mrs Williams

Thank you for your latest letter. I look forward to sitting down one day to No Frills Pate De Foie Gras with a glass of No Frills Chateau Petrus claret. I think if you were to keep the price of the former down to about the cost of Sutherland's Ham and Tongue Spread and the price of the wine to around £4 a bottle you could well have a couple of very popular lines.

Now we have got the starter and the wine sorted out, how about introducing a No Frills Escargots de Conserve a la Bourguignon for the main course?

Yours faithfully

T Ravenscroft (Mr)

*

KWIK SAVE

Our Ref: GHW/MW/2999
17th July

Mr Ravenscroft
17 Lingland Road
New Mills
Cheshire

Dear Mr Ravenscroft

No Frills Escargots De Conserve A La Bourguignon

Thank you for your recent letter regarding the possibility of stocking the above products in Kwik Save stores. Kwik Save's aim is to provide loyal customers with the best value shopping basket anywhere. As we trade from units which are usually smaller than most of our competitors, we must pay constant attention not only to market trends but also to our customers when assessing store ranges. We carry out reviews at regular intervals and your suggestion will be considered at our next review meeting.

We do appreciate our customer's taking the time to make constructive suggestions which will improve the range of products and services we offer. Please do not hesitate to advise us of any other product you feel would be a worthwhile addition to our range.

Yours sincerely

G H Williams (Mrs)

****

                                                17 Lingland Road
                                                        New Mills
                                                        CHESHIRE

                                                        28th March

J Sainsburys PLC
Stockport

Dear J Sainsburys

Reference you advertisement for New Zealand Lamb in The Sunday Times Magazine, today's date, in which you say you will 'Refund your money in full if your taste buds aren't delighted.' Well last Saturday I purchased a joint of your New Zealand

Lamb, which we had for Sunday lunch along with our usual oven chips, and whilst my taste buds were by no means offended they were certainly not delighted. I must point out here that my taste buds are in fine working order. Proof of this, if proof were needed, is that as I enjoy a Big Mac as much as anyone.

I would also point out that we gave the remains of the joint to our dog Rantzen and it made him sick - although it must be said that along with the lamb we gave him a few sprouts which had been tossed in 'I Can't Believe It's Not Butter', so that may very well have had something to do with it.

However, taking both opinions into consideration, mine and the dog's, it would seem that by the terms of your advertisement I am due for my money back . Could you please therefore let me know how I go about getting it?

Yours faithfully
T Ravenscroft (Mr)

*

17 Lingland Road
New Mills
CHESHIRE

10th April

Richard Bewley
Meat Manager
J Sainsburys PLC
Stockport

Dear Richard Bewley

Thank you for telephoning yesterday to apologise for your very ordinary New Zealand Lamb, and your offer to recompense me.

My wife can't remember exactly how much she paid for it – she's like that with money - but she said it was 'ten pounds or thereabouts'. (She'd have known if she'd had to earn the money to pay for it!) As I am a man of some means I don't really need the refund so I would be grateful if you could donate it to Cancer Research, with my best wishes.

Yours faithfully

T Ravenscroft (Mr)

****

17 Lingland Road
New Mills
CHESHIRE

1st April

The Ryvita Company Ltd
Poole
Dorset

Dear Ryvita

Despite being in my forties I have just tried Ryvita for the very first time. What a revelation! Since first sampling them not much more than a week ago I have already devoured six packets! I eat them two at a time thickly spread with butter with about a dozen oven chips in-between as part of a calorie-controlled diet. The only fault I find with them is that they tend to make the roof of my mouth sore. Would your Oat Bran or Dark Rye versions be any more forgiving?

Yours faithfully

T Ravenscroft (Mr)

*

RYVITA

24 April
Mr T Ravenscroft
17 Lingland Road
New Mills
CHESHIRE

Dear Mr Ravenscroft

Thank you for your letter of 1st April and please accept my sincere apologies for the delay in responding.

We are absolutely delighted that you have discovered Ryvita and are intrigued at a calorie controlled diet which includes regular helpings of Ryvita Chip Butties!

With reference to your particular queries, Ryvita is 100% natural and doesn't contain artificial additives or preservatives. The ingredients are purely wholemeal rye, water and a pinch of salt. Ryvita is therefore naturally high in fibre and low in fat and contains a natural balance of vitamins and minerals. As such, Ryvita is the ideal product to be incorporated into any healthy eating plan and is widely recommended by nutritionists and slimming clubs. However, if you are generally concerned about your diet, we would recommend that you see your doctor who is the best person to advise you on the suitability of your diet.

As Ryvita is baked at fairly high temperatures, it is naturally very crunchy but there are many toppings you can use to help soften the crispbread which are also delicious and very nutritious. We have enclosed some booklets on Ryvita toppings and serving suggestions to give you some ideas. In addition, we also manufacture an extruded crispbread called 'Crackerbread'. Crackerbread has a 'softer' bite than Ryvita and we are enclosing a pack for you to try. Crackerbread, like Ryvita, is available from all major multiples.

We do hope this gives you lots of ideas and good luck with the diet.

With kind regards

Yours sincerely

Cathy Dalton
Product Manager

17 Lingland Road
New Mills
CHESHIRE

Cathy Dalton
The Ryvita Company Ltd
Poole

Dear Cathy Dalton

Thank you for your letter of 24th April and the packets of Crackerbread. Thank you also for the booklets, especially the No Diet Diet. At the time of writing I have been on your Daily Dash breakfast for a week, and by now I know why you've called it the Daily Dash. I'm going to try your Pack up and Go next week and if its name turns out to be equally appropriate I am certainly not going to forget where the lavatory is. I have also tried Tempting Tuna and can report that if you cut out the low calorie mayonnaise and replace it with a generous portion of oven chips it is even more tempting. You might like to include it when you compile your next booklet? You could call it Tempting Providence.

Yours faithfully

T Ravenscroft (Mr)

NO REPLY!

****

17 Lingland Road
New Mills
CHESHIRE

2nd April
H J Heinz Co Ltd
Hayes
Middlesex

Dear H J Heinz

I am afraid that I have a rather serious complaint to make about your Thomas the Tank Engine and Friends Pasta Shapes.

81

Yesterday I opened a can of this concoction for my youngest's lunch. On giving it to him he immediately went a bright shade of red and started screaming. Then, completely without warning, he hurled the entire contents of the bowl at the kitchen wall.

I would respectfully point out that on the can it clearly states that the pasta shapes contained within include, amongst others, Thomas the Tank Engine, Harold the Helicopter, Trevor the Tractor and The Fat Controller. My complaint, and the reason for my two-year-old's eccentric behaviour, is that the can didn't contain so much as a single Fat Controller, which happens to be young Oscar's favourite. (He likes to bite his head off) You can take the can's lack of Fat Controllers as gospel, as I had to remove every one of the sixty five pasta pieces from the kitchen wall. For what it's worth, I counted twenty two Thomas the Tank Engines, eleven Harold the Helicopters, seven Trevor the Tractors, ten Bertie the Buses, nine unspecified items which slightly resembled bridges or signal boxes, and six unspecified items which were unidentifiable but certainly weren't the Fat Controller, at least not unless Thomas the Tank Engine had just run over him.

From the time I placed the bowl of Thomas the Tank Engine and Friends Pasta Shapes in front of Oscar until the time I had restored the kitchen floor to its former pristine condition, including settling down Oscar and cleaning the kitchen wall, took up an hour of my valuable time. This was completely due to your negligence and I would like to know what you intend to do about it?

Yours faithfully

T Ravenscroft (Mr)

Heinz

Mr T Ravenscroft
17 Lingland Road
New Mills

Dear Mr Ravenscroft

Thank you for letting us know all about your experience with our Thomas The Tank Spaghetti.

We are concerned to learn that one of our products did not meet our normal high standards. The greatest care is taken to ensure that our products reach our customers in perfect condition and tests are carried out by our staff at every stage during preparation and manufacture. Our procedures are approved and regularly audited by independent authorities. It is apparent from your comments, however, that a filling fault has occurred in this instance.

As you would expect, we take our responsibilities to our customers very seriously indeed. Thank you for your help in supplying information about your complaint: this is used to help us in our programme of continuous improvement of our equipment and quality procedures.

We are sorry you have had this experience with our product. Please accept the enclosed in accordance with our guarantee to refund the price of the product if it does not meet your requirements. We hope your confidence in our products has been restored and that we will continue to receive your valued custom.

Yours sincerely,

Helen Reeves, Consumer Contact

17 Lingland Road
New Mills
CHESHIRE

12th April

Your ref 0335827A
Helen Reeves
H J Heinz Co Ltd
Hayes
Middlesex

Dear Helen Reeves

Thank you for your letter of 8th April.

It is nice to know that you take such care in ensuring that your products reach your customers in the best of condition. Unfortunately I am having great difficulty in believing you. The reason for this is your inexplicable reference to 'Thomas the Tank'. I would respectfully point out to you that Thomas is not a tank, but a tank engine. It seems to me that if you at Heinz can't tell the difference between a tank and a tank engine then there is not much chance of you being able to tell the difference between Bertie the Bus and The Fat Controller, and if this is the case you are going to have many more cans lacking Fat Controllers. I just hope that I am not unfortunate enough to serve up one of them to young Oscar, or it will be kitchen wall cleaning time again!

Which brings me to the voucher for £2 that you enclosed, which I am returning to you as I regard it as an insult. If this was meant to compensate me for the time I spent cleaning my kitchen then it is totally inadequate. Good Lord woman, it cost me almost that much in Flash alone.

For the record, a tank is a large military vehicle, which runs on tracks and has a big gun at the front. A tank engine is a wheeled traction vehicle used on the railway to pull carriages.

Yours faithfully

T Ravenscroft (Mr)

*

Heinz

Mr T Ravenscroft
17 Lingland Road
New Mills
CHESHIRE

Dear Mr Ravenscroft

We were sorry to learn that you are unhappy with our original response to your complaint about a lack of 'Fat Controllers' in a tin of Thomas the Tank Engine and Friends Pasta Shapes.

We note that you were unhappy with our reimbursement. However it is our policy to ensure that all our consumers are refunded for any product which they feel does not meet their expectations. Our vouchers were intended to reflect this and we are sorry you chose not to accept them.

Yours sincerely,

Brian Hooker
Consumer Contact Manager

17 Lingland Road
New Mills
CHESHIRE

Your ref 0335827A

Brian Hooker
H J Heinz Co Ltd

86

Hayes
Middlesex

Dear Brian Hooker

The reason I found your original response inadequate was not because I was unhappy about you reimbursement - I am not a man who seeks nor needs charity - but because you at Heinz don't seem to know the difference between a tank and a tank engine. I really expected more from one of our leading food manufacturers.

I have now realised why you came up with the slogan 'Heinz 57 Varieties'. It is quite obviously some legal ploy – 'varieties' being a suitably vague enough expression to cater for the eccentricities of your can filling machinery, and 57 of them to cover you in the event of your mistaking a tank engine for any of 56 other large locomotives.

Yours faithfully

T Ravenscroft (Mr)

NO REPLY!

****

17 Lingland Road
New Mills
CHESHIRE

Interpet Ltd
Dorking

Dear Interpet

As a fishpond owner I am never without a supply of your product 3 Seasons Floating Food Hoops. The other day my wife accidentally served a portion of them to my middle son Henry, in mistake for Kellogg's Honey Nut Loops, which are very similar in appearance. Far from complaining about it, Henry wolfed down the lot, and with even more gusto than usual, then enquired as to what the 'super new breakfast cereal' was and could he have it regularly.

I must say that I don't share my son's opinion of the taste of your Floating Food Hoops - I tried a spoonful, and to me they taste like rabbit hutches - but then what appeals to the palate of a child has never ceased to amaze me since the advent of the fish finger and the Big Mac. However, the way I see it is that if he wants to eat fish food that's his kettle of fish - or rather his bowl of 3 Seasons Floating Food Hoops - so good luck to him. Before I give him my blessing however I thought it would be prudent to check with you to ensure that there isn't anything in your product which might be harmful to human children. I look forward to hearing from you.

Yours faithfully

T Ravenscroft (Mr)

17 Lingland Road
New Mills
CHESHIRE

28th April

Interpet Ltd
Dorking
Surrey

88

Dear Interpet

I would refer you to a letter that I sent to you on 8th April. I really expected an answer before now. Indeed, if my Japanese Koi fish had to wait as long for their 3 Seasons Floating Food Hoops as I have had to wait for an answer from you they would have become 'floaters' long ago. So please, as my boy Henry is back on the Kellogg's Honey Nut Loops again and consequently is making my life a misery with his pestering.

Yours faithfully

T Ravenscroft (Mr)

*

INTERPET

6th May
JEP/cc
Mr T Ravenscroft
17 Lingland Road
New Mills
Cheshire

Dear Mr Ravenscroft

Thank you for your recent correspondence and we would offer our apologies for the delay in responding to you. Unfortunately, our research scientist has been absent from the office and we needed to clarify the situation with him.

Although the product is harmless, we cannot advise or recommend it for human consumption. We would therefore suggest that Henry continues with Kellogg's Honey Nut Loops.

Once again, please accept our apologies for the delay.

Yours sincerely

Julie Parker
Customer Services Administrator

17 Lingland Road
New Mills
CHESHIRE

Julie Parker
Interpet Ltd
Dorking

Dear Julie Parker

Thank you for your letter of 6th May.

Since writing to you there has been a development. Apparently Henry has been eating your Floating Food Hoops behind my back ever since I first wrote to you on 8th April! It appears that the young shaver has been taking a handful out of the container into which I dole the daily ration for feeding to my Koi, then mixing it in with his Honey Nut Loops. (I only found out when I became suspicious because the fish always seemed to be hungry). When I showed him your letter he begged me to disregard it, and pleaded with me to be allowed to continue eating Floating Food Hoops, pointing out that he hasn't suffered any ill effects, so why not? In fact he has never looked fitter, and he swears that his swimming has improved, although whether that is due to eating fish food or just that he is a growing lad is debatable.

Bearing the above in mind I am loathe to stop him eating Floating Fish Hoops, and to this end I would be interested to know why you can't recommend them for human consumption if, as you say, they are harmless?

Yours faithfully

T Ravenscroft (Mr)

*

INTERPET

20th May
JEP/cc
Mr T Ravenscroft
17 Lingland Road
New Mills
91

Cheshire

Dear Mr Ravenscroft

Thank you for your further letter dated 8 May regarding our Floating Food Hoops.

We are delighted that Henry enjoys the product so much! However, we can only reiterate what we stated in our previous letter. There are obviously very differing regulations laid down in the production, packaging and handling of food for human consumption as against food for animal or fish consumption. As far as we are concerned, there is nothing in the product which would be harmful if consumed by a human but we cannot recommend it since it was not produced for this purpose nor has it passed the stringent tests to pronounce it fit for human consumption.

We are sorry that we cannot be more helpful.

Yours sincerely
Julie Parker
Customer Services Administrator

*

17 Lingland Road
New Mills
CHESHIRE

23rd May

Julie Parker
Interpet Ltd
Dorking

Surrey

Dear Julie Parker

Thank you for your letter of 20th May.

Henry continues to enjoy Floating Food Hoops mixed in equal proportions with his Kellogg's Honey Nut Loops. My wife swears that he is developing scales on his lower left leg but it's just a particularly bad case of athlete's foot if you ask me.

Thank you for all your help.

Yours faithfully

T Ravenscroft (Mr)

****

17 Lingland Road
New Mills
CHESHIRE

12th April

Cadbury Ltd
Bournville
Birmingham

Dear Cadbury

Might I congratulate you on the position you have taken with regard to product placement, since taking on the mantle of Coronation Street's sponsor. It would have been all too easy for you to put pressure on the programme's producers to include in each episode gratuitous close-ups of your products, but I can honestly say I have yet to see so much as a Chocolate Button on my favourite soap! Given the more liberal attitude to sex taken by the producers of Coronation Street nowadays, it would have been all too easy to feature shots of Deirdre nibbling a Milk Flake or Liz sucking a Walnut Whip, but no, your restraint has been admirable. I take my hat off to you.

Yours faithfully

T Ravenscroft (Mr)

*

Cadbury

Our ref; L17/CD/SF
Mr T Ravenscroft
17 Lingland Road
New Mills

Cheshire

Dear Mr Ravenscroft

Thank you very much for your letter dated 12th April concerning the Cadbury sponsorship of Coronation Street.

I thank you for your kind words concerning our sponsorship, as you correctly state it would be quite improper of us to influence the programme in any way, be it having our products included, or trying to influence the story lines of the show.

I note however that you say it would be easy to feature shots of a Flake or a Walnut Whip, but I can assure you that as we do not produce Walnut Whip that is one product we would certainly be trying not to get featured! Once again thank you for taking the trouble to write to us.

Yours Sincerely

Carol Dunseith, Consumer Services Manager

*

17 Lingland Road
New Mills
CHESHIRE
24th April

Your ref L17/CD/SF

Carol Dunseith
Cadbury Ltd

PO Box 12
Bournville

Dear Carol Dunseith

It's Sod's Law, isn't it! No sooner do I congratulate you on your restraint than you go and blot your copybook. I refer of course to last Monday's episode of Coronation Street when Emily was to be seen looking longingly at a Mars Bar in the Corner Shop. Let's hope that this was just a temporary lapse!

My apologies for thinking that you make Walnut Whips. They are certainly good enough to be made by Cadbury. Who makes them?

Yours faithfully

T Ravenscroft (Mr)

*

Cadbury

Our Ref:- O33623lB JAP
29th April

Mr T Ravenscroft
17 Lingland Road

New Mills
Cheshire

Dear Mr Ravenscroft

Thank you for your letter dated 24th April concerning Cadbury products on Coronation Street.

I was sorry to learn that you feel we have now blotted our copybook because Emily looked longingly at a Mars Bar in one episode last week. Cadbury do not produce Mars Bars these are made by Mars. But now that a Mars Bar has been featured, I do hope you will feel it is only fair if one of our products does appear in the future!

In answer to your question concerning Walnut Whips these are made by Nestle. I note you think they are good enough to be made by Cadbury's, but I don't think their chocolate is as nice as ours - but I would say that wouldn't I!

Thank you for writing to us.

Yours Sincerely

Carol Dunseith
Consumer Services Manager

*

17 Lingland Road
New Mills
CHESHIRE

2nd May

Your ref 0336231B JAP

97

Carol Dunseith
Cadbury Ltd
PO Box 12
Bournville

Thank you for your letter of 29th April.

You are right, it would only be fair if one of your products were
to appear in a future episode of Coronation Street. I don't know
whether or not you have any influence with the scriptwriters, but
a scene with Norris balancing Smarties on Rita's nipples then
flicking them off into a Cadburys Chocolate Easter Egg held by
Tyrone Dobbs might go down well. What do you think?

Yours faithfully

T Ravenscroft (Mr)

NO REPLY!

****

17 Lingland Road
New Mills
CHESHIRE

6th March

Nestle
98

Customer Services
PO Box 207
York

Dear Nescafe

Whilst I was on holiday in America just recently I came across Power Coffee, a beverage which contains 50% extra caffeine. Naturally I tried it as I'm a man who can't get enough caffeine and I regularly drinking ten or more cups of coffee a day. I've heard it claimed by do-gooders that consuming a lot of caffeine isn't good for you but it's never done me any harm. I can report that Power Coffee was quite wonderful; a cup of it not so much lifted me as picked me up, gave me a good shaking and inspired me to get out there and kick ass, as the Americans say.

Unfortunately I have a weak bladder and need the toilet a lot, which isn't always convenient as I am long distance lorry driver - or perhaps I should say I am a short distance lorry driver who eventually drives a long distance seeing as I have to keep stopping to go to the toilet, ha ha - but drinking Power Coffee when I was in America meant that I could drink only half as many cups of coffee for just as much caffeine, and consequently I didn't have to go to the toilet as much. In fact I only had to go once the whole five hours we spent in Disney World whereas the previous time I went there I had to go four times, and one of those times was behind the Enchanted Castle as I couldn't find a toilet, which greatly embarrassed me.

Is it possible that you at Nescafe sell a version of Power Coffee? I am not hopeful as I've never seen it on the shelves at Tescos and they sell just about everything, but there's no harm in asking, is there?

Yours sincerely

T Ravenscroft (Mr)

*

Nestle

Mr T Ravenscroft
17 Lingland Road
New Mills
CHESHIRE

001874979 A4 March

Dear Mr Ravenscroft

Thank you for your recent letter.

Unfortunately Power Coffee is not available for sale in the United Kingdom. Whilst sales do well in America, consumer research suggests that demand for it in the UK would not be sufficient to justify the long production runs necessary to ensure the good value customers require.

Our experience with this and other brands leads us to conclude that consumer tastes can vary considerably between different countries. Nescafe Fine Blend contains 4.6g of caffeine. Per 100g jar, 1 teaspoon is roughly 3g.

We hope that this reply is not too disappointing. However, our marketing policy is constantly under review and your comments have been noted.

As I am sure you will appreciate, we receive many requests for information and we are not always able to go into great detail on the specific points raised. However, we enclose a booklet all about coffee which we hope you will find helpful.

Thank you once again for taking the trouble to contact us and for the interest you have shown in our Company.

Yours sincerely

Sue Tomlinson
Customer Service Executive
Consumer Service

*

17 Lingland Road
New Mills
CHESHIRE

17th March

Sue Tomlinson
Customer Service Executive
Nestle
PO Box 207
York

Dear Sue Tomlinson

Thank you for your letter. Shame that you don't do Power Coffee over here but I'll survive I suppose, it was just that the less I have to go to the toilet for a pee the better I like it, as sometimes toilets aren't readily available.

However I've had an idea. Do you think if I were to make a batch of your coffee, say a gallon, and boil it down to half a gallon that it would double the caffeine content? Have a word with your boffins and let me know, would you?

Thank you also for the four wonderful booklets all about coffee that you sent to me, especially the one entitled The Power of Love, all about the Gold Blend couple Sharon and Tony. What a love story! I was an avid follower at the time, although I must say that my wife thought it was a bit soppy, but then that's about all you can expect from an ex-lady wrestler.

I think you were wise not to mention that since drinking all that coffee Sharon died rather prematurely in Holby City. If you had done some people might have thought it had something to do with your coffee, which I'm sure it wasn't, but you can't stop people from talking, can you.

Looking forward to hearing from you.

Yours sincerely

T Ravenscroft (Mr)

*

Nestle

Mr T Ravenscroft
17 Lingland Road
New Mills
CHESHIRE
001874978   21March

Dear Mr Ravenscroft

Thank you for your recent letter concerning coffee.

With reference to your question, caffeine melts at 238 degrees centigrade. It doesn't boil, but sublimes at 178 degs. So if you wanted to concentrate some solubilised coffee to half its volume, the caffeine concentration would approximately double as the temperature required to boil coffee mixture is only just over 100 degs.

Thank you once again for taking the trouble to contact us and for the interest you have shown in our Company.

Yours sincerely

Melanie Durkin
Customer Relations Officer, Consumer Services

*

17 Lingland Road
New Mills
CHESHIRE

29th March

Melanie Durkin
Customer Relations Officer

Nestle
PO Box 207
York

Dear Mel

Thanks for the useful information. I wasted no time in making a batch of Power Coffee. At first I was going to boil two gallons of coffee down to one gallon to give me a beverage with 100% added caffeine, but, never a man to go about things half-heartedly, I decided to distil the two gallons down to a bit under two pints, giving me a concoction which had a caffeine content of an extra 1000%.

What a brew! To try it out I mixed a generous helping into our dog Rantzen's Pedigree Chum - I have absolutely nothing against experimenting on animals - and it didn't stop barking for two days. Then I tried it myself and realised what all the fuss was about.

I realise of course that caffeine stimulates the central nervous system, which is why I can't get enough of it, as I like to be stimulated, but I can honestly say that my central nervous system was stimulated beyond my wildest dreams. I drank just one mug full of it on Monday morning and I haven't been to bed since and today is Thursday. During that time I have worked three shifts, driving over eight hundred miles (with no pit stops to go to the toilet, no small thanks to you), decorated our living room, dug the foundations for an extension, tarred the garage roof, twice run ten miles in training for the next London Marathon, made love four times and dug a dog's grave.

This stuff should be on prescription and I urge you to consider adding it to your range. It would be criminal not to.

Finally, I am looking for sponsors for when I take part in the London Marathon. All monies donated will go to good causes. Possibly towards a stone for Sharon of the Gold Blend ads if she hasn't already got one. Can I put you down for say, a hundred pounds?

Yours sincerely

T Ravenscroft (Mr)

*

Nestle

Mr T Ravenscroft
17 Lingland Road
New Mills
CHESHIRE

Dear Mr Ravenscroft

Thank you for your recent enquiry.

As I am sure you will appreciate, we receive many requests every year for financial or product donations. We were able to support over 20% of the fifteen thousand requests last year and the total donated was £1,000,000. Although we would like to help everyone it is obviously not possible to do so.

We have considered your request for sponsorship very carefully but we are advised by our colleagues in Marketing that we are currently not able to support this idea.

The aim of the Nestle Trust is to invest in partnerships and programmes which support the Nutrition, Health and Wellness

105

of young people and which really make a positive difference to their lives. We tend to focus on local good causes which are well managed and relevant to the company and where support will create goodwill with the community generally.

The key area for support is young people (specifically teenagers 11-18 year olds) in the following areas: Out of school childcare generally and specifically 4Children and Make Space, Nutrition, Health and Wellness, Sport, Education (but not areas which are the responsibility of the Local Education Authority), Community Development.

Because of the number of requests we receive, we focus our support on charities or good causes which are local to our factories, and, where appropriate, make a donation direct. Thank you for taking the time and trouble to contact us and for giving us the opportunity to explain our position. I wish you every success in your fund-raising efforts.

Yours sincerely

Melanie Durkin
Consumer Relations Officer
Consumer Services.

*

17 Lingland Road
New Mills
CHESHIRE

24th April

Melanie Durkin
Customer Relations Officer
Nestle

York

Dear Mel

Last Sunday, fuelled by Nescafe 1000% extra caffeine as recommended by your good self, I ran in the London Marathon. Sadly you didn't feel able to sponsor me for this event, but I don't hold this against you, in fact quite the opposite, otherwise I wouldn't have had the words 'Nescafe Made This Possible' emblazoned on my running singlet. Did you perhaps get a glimpse of me? I was running just behind Rod Hull and Emu for a couple of miles (I wasn't chancing running in front of him after what he did to Michael Parkinson!). I am told by friends that I was briefly on television three times, which is excellent publicity for Nescafe I am sure.

It was my hope of course to complete the course, but sadly this proved to be a little too much for me. However I covered twelve and a half miles before I collapsed, which is almost halfway, and raised £433. In fact I am fairly sure the TV cameras were on me when I lost consciousness. I am *absolutely* sure they were on me when a St John's Ambulance man revived me at the side of the road because the cameraman asked him to move to one side so he could get a good shot of me. You will be happy to know that even though I was still quite groggy I had the presence of mind to point at the 'Nescafe Made This Possible' motto on my singlet.

In view of this would you like to reconsider your decision not to sponsor me?

Yours sincerely

T Ravenscroft (Mr)

*

Nestle

Mr T Ravenscroft
17 Lingland Road
New Mills

Dear Mr Ravenscroft

Thank you for your recent letter. Congratulations on your marvellous effort in the London Marathon and for raising £433.00. We were sorry to learn that you failed to complete the course and hope you are now fully recovered. Further to our previous letter, in which we said we were unable to sponsor you, there has been no change in our decision. Sorry if this response is disappointing for you.

Thank you once again for your interest in our products.

Yours sincerely

Gillian Liddell
Consumer Relations Officer, Customer Services.

****

17 Lingland Road
New Mills
CHESHIRE
1st May

Hovis Ltd
Yorkley

Dear Hovis

There are a number of Bovis homes under construction not far from where I live. As I passed by the other day the bricklayers and their labourers were on their their lunch break. I observed that each and every one of them was eating sandwiches made with Hovis bread. Now I realise of course that Hovis is popular, but ten men all eating it is too much of a coincidence, and I got to wondering if there is any connection between Hovis and Bovis, their names being so similar, and that the workers were maybe getting subsidised bread. Could I be right? Is Bovis indeed a subsidiary of Hovis? Incidentally, each of the workers was a fine figure of a man and a testament to your bread, with not so much an inch of buttock cleavage between them as far as I could discern.

Yours faithfully

T Ravenscroft (Mr)

*

KEARS GROUP LTD

12th May,
Mr Ravenscroft
17 Lingland Road
New Mills
Cheshire

Dear Mr Ravenscroft

Thank you for your letter re Hovis bread and Bovis Homes, we would like to confirm that:

THE TWO ARE NOT CONNECTED
GOOD BREAD'S OUR CLAIM TO FAME
BUILDING HOUSES JUST AREN'T US
BRICKS JUST DON'T TASTE THE SAME
THE REASON PEOPLE EAT IT
BE THEY BUILDERS FIT OR NOT
IS THE TASTE THE TEXTURE AND HEALTHINESS
WITH HOVIS YOU GET THE LOT.

I hope this clears up your questions regarding Hovis Bread, but should you require any further information please do not hesitate to contact me.

Yours Sincerely

KEARS GROUP LTD

L. Childs (Mrs)
Quality Assurance Department

*

17 Lingland Road
New Mills
CHESHIRE

19th May

L Childs (Mrs)
Kears Group
Lydney
Glos

Dear L Childs (Mrs)

Thank you for your letter of 12th May. What an original and entertaining reply! Since I wrote to you I have become quite friendly with the workers building the Bovis homes, and have discovered that most of them don't in fact eat Hovis bread, and what I took to be your bread was actually other brands of brown bread, notably Allinsons Stone Ground and Warburtons. It is ironic then that the only one of them who does eat Hovis, Declan his name is, is the least healthy-looking of the lot of them, having a definite hump back and a limp, although this could well be to do with him carrying a hod all day.

Although Hovis may be trailing a little behind the others in its health-giving properties I can report that it could very well make people poetic, because after I showed Declan your letter he immediately offered the following ditty.

EAT BROWN BREAD
SHIT LIKE LEAD
NO BLOODY WONDER
FART LIKE THUNDER
EAT BROWN BREAD

I like to think of myself as a bit of a poet, but I am nowhere near as adept at the art as your good self and Declan, so with this in mind I am seriously considering changing to Hovis in the hope that it will improve my poems. I'll let you know if it does.

Yours faithfully

T Ravenscroft (Mr)

****

17 Lingland Road
New Mills
CHESHIRE

26th March

Van den Bergh Foods Ltd
Brooke House
Crawley
West Sussex

112

Dear Van den Bergh Foods

I have just tried a packet of your 'I Can't Believe It's Not Butter!' After sampling it I very soon came to the conclusion that whoever thought up the name for your product may have been guilty of setting his sights a little too high. I suggest that a more appropriate and believable name might have been 'I Can't Believe It's Not Vegetable Oils, Buttermilk, Water, Salt, Milk Proteins, Lactic Acid, Emulsifier, Nono and Di Gycerides, Lecithin, Preservative, Sorbic Acid, Vitamins A, D and E, Flavouring, Colour and Natural Carotene', which is what it actually is, or at least that's what it claims on the wrapper. Perhaps 'I Can't Believe It's Not Axle Grease', which is what it actually tastes like?

Who are these odd people who 'Can't Believe It's Not Butter'? A special race who have their taste buds removed at puberty?

It is my intention to report your spurious claim to the authorities unless you can give me one good reason why I shouldn't.

Yours faithfully

T Ravenscroft (Mr)

*

Van den Bergh Foods

April 15
Mr T Ravenscroft
17 Lingland Road
New Mills
CHESHIRE

Dear Mr Ravenscroft

Thank you for your recent letter from which we were most concerned to learn that you were disappointed with your purchase of a tub of I Can't Believe It's Not Butter!

Before any products are launched by us on a national scale, they are first test marketed in one or two areas for a long period of time. In this way we are able to collect all kinds of consumer reaction to the product, the type and design of packaging and, of course, texture and taste but we do appreciate that taste is a matter of personal preference.

In view of the above, we are very sorry that you have been disappointed. We would, however, like to thank you for the interest you have shown in our product.

Yours sincerely
Jayne Pratt, Customer Services Manager

*

17 Lingland Road
New Mills
CHESHIRE

18th April

Your ref 0059336A

Jayne Pratt
Van den Bergh Foods Ltd
Crawley
West Sussex

Dear Jayne Pratt

Thank you for your letter of 15th April.

You are correct, taste is indeed a personal preference. It was therefore with some surprise that I noted your company motto on your letter heading reads 'In touch with people's tastes'. By your own admission - 'that taste is a personal preference' - this is a false statement. To be truthful and meaningful your motto should be 'In touch with some people's taste', or, even more truthfully, 'In touch with the taste of people who haven't got any taste'. I also couldn't help noticing that you have a Royal Warrant to supply Her Majesty The Queen with Low Fat Spreads and Margarine. No wonder she always looks miserable.

Yours faithfully

T Ravenscroft (Mr)

*

17 Lingland Road
New Mills
CHESHIRE

14th April

John West Foods Ltd
Bixteth Street
Liverpool

Dear John West

I am suffering from a personal medical condition of which I will spare you the details. However my doctor says it might help if I cut down on my salt intake. Unfortunately I just love anchovies, and especially John West Anchovies in Olive Oil, which are, of course, extremely salty. I really wouldn't like to forego my daily tin of anchovies if it can be avoided, and with this in mind I was wondering if you do a low salt or salt free version?

Yours faithfully

T Ravenscroft (Mr)

*

JOHN WEST

Mr T Ravenscroft
17 Lingland Road
New Mills
Cheshire

Dear Mr Ravenscroft

Thank you for your letter of 14th April.

I regret that we do not do a low salt or salt free anchovy. It is important to have the right salt levels to preserve the product and therefore a free salt version would have to be a fully retorted product becoming a product like Brisling or Sardines.

I am sorry therefore we cannot help at this time.

Yours sincerely

KEITH WILSON
MARKET MANAGER

*

17 Lingland Road
New Mills
CHESHIRE
24th April

Keith Wilson
John West Foods Ltd
Liverpool

Dear Keith Wilson

Thank you for your letter of 21sth April.

It seems that in order to enlist your help I will have to come clean about my personal medical condition. Your being a man is a big help, God knows what I would have done had you been a woman. The thing is I am having trouble 'performing', if you know what I mean. Now I like sex as much as I like anchovies, so you can imagine my dilemma. With this in mind, perhaps you can see your way to helping me?

It looks like I will have to obtain some 'fully retorted' anchovies, whatever that means. If I could get hold of some anchovies would I be able to fully retort them myself? I look forward to hearing from you.

Yours faithfully
T Ravenscroft (Mr)

*

JOHN WEST

Mr T Ravenscroft
17 Lingland Road
New Mills
Cheshire

Dear Mr Ravenscroft

Thank you for your further letter of 24th April. I am sorry to learn of your problem but do not feel we can be of any further assistance. The raw material is caught and processed in Spain, Portugal, Italy, Morocco and South America and therefore we do not receive raw material here in the UK.

I can only suggest you soak the current pack of Anchovies in milk to lessen the salt content which may make the product acceptable to your dilemma.

Yours sincerely

KEITH WILSON
MARKET MANAGER

*

17 Lingland Road
New Mills
CHESHIRE

12th May

Keith Wilson
John West Foods Ltd
Liverpool

Dear Keith Wilson

Thank you for your letter of 29th April.

I am trying your idea of soaking your anchovies in milk but thus far it has only been a partial success, inasmuch as that although it satisfies my craving for anchovies I am still unable to fulfil my marital obligations. Up to now.

I have something quite odd to report. Rather than waste the milk in which the anchovies have soaked, I have been putting it down for the cat, and what only a few weeks ago was a shagged-out old tom now has a definite glint in his eye and has taken to stopping out all night again. He has never had anchovy flavoured milk before of course, and there is no doubt in my mind that it is this which has perked him up.

I'll let you know if there are any developments as you might be on to a winner here.

In the meantime it has occurred to me that where John West's Anchovies in Olive Oil is concerned there are no economies to be made. What I mean is that when I buy beans I buy them in big cans, which are more economical than small cans. So given my passion for anchovies I would prefer to buy bigger cans of them, thus saving myself some money. Why isn't this possible?

Yours faithfully

T Ravenscroft (Mr)

*

JOHN WEST

KW/DLF
14th May
Mr T Ravenscroft
17 Lingland Road
New Mills
Cheshire

Dear Mr Ravenscroft

The final bit of help I can give you is to advise that we have just launched a l00g Anchovies in Glass Jar.

These will shortly be available in Tesco and Sainsburys and hopefully other stores as we continue to launch this product.

Yours sincerely

KEITH WILSON
MARKET MANAGER

*

17 Lingland Road
New Mills
CHESHIRE

Keith Wilson
John West Foods Ltd
Liverpool

Dear Keith Wilson

I am sorry to hear that you are leaving John West, and thank you for the final bit of advice you were able to give me. Good luck with your new job. I enclose a small donation of five pounds towards your leaving present.

Unfortunately I have refused to shop at Sainsburys, ever since they made wild claims about the quality of their New Zealand Lamb, and I'm not on very good terms with Tesco either, so I won't be able to take advantage of your 100g Anchovies in Glass Jar. Perhaps your successor could advise me of any other outlets you are considering?

I am persisting with the milk-soaked anchovies and I am definitely feeling a bit friskier. It looks like this could turn out to be the best tip I have ever had, particularly as the cat is going from strength to strength on anchovy-flavoured milk, and has got the corner shop's tabby pregnant, according to the owner, Mr Singh.

Thank you for all your help.

Yours faithfully
T Ravenscroft (Mr)

*

JOHN WEST

KW/DLF
22 May
Mr T Ravenscroft
17 Lingland Road
New Mills
Cheshire

Dear Mr Ravenscroft
121

Thank you very much for your cheque for £5 but there is a misunderstanding as I am not leaving John West.

I therefore return your kind donation and wish you well for the future.

Yours sincerely
KEITH WILSON
MARKET MANAGER

*

17 Lingland Road
New Mills
CHESHIRE

Keith Wilson
John West Foods Ltd
Liverpool

Dear Keith Wilson

Sorry about the misunderstanding, but because you said in your letter of 14th May that it was the final bit of help you could give me I naturally assumed you were leaving John West's, as I found it difficult to believe that someone who had previously been so helpful would suddenly refuse to give help, especially to a good customer.

Anyway I'm glad we've got it sorted out because you now may be able to help me in a big way, as your idea of soaking anchovies in milk is proving to be the best idea since sliced bread. I have only been on them for four weeks and already I can fulfil my marital obligations, and then some! In fact my wife says it's like being on honeymoon again. (I hope not because I got her pregnant!) When you also take into account what has happened to our cat, who continues to terrorise the neighbourhood's feline population, there can be little doubt that milk-soaked anchovies possess outstanding aphrodisiac qualities. This is bound to be of tremendous interest to lovers of anchovies and lovers of sex alike, and even those who don't like the former could very well be prepared to put up with them if they gave them a sporting chance of getting more of the latter.

Bearing in mind the above, I am considering marketing Milk-Soaked Anchovies as a sex aid, and I would be grateful to you if you could like you to let me know your best price for anchovies in 100 kg barrels, or whatever they come in; or failing that the name of your suppliers abroad so that I can do business with them direct.

Yours faithfully

T Ravenscroft (Mr)

NO REPLY!

****

17 Lingland Road
New Mills
CHESHIRE

25th March

Mars UK
Slough

Dear Mars

I have recently heard of the quite amazing phenomenon of Deep Fried Mars Bars. My wife and I have long been fans of Mars Bars, and buy at least ten each per week, but we've certainly never had them deep-fried. As we are most anxious to try them this way - it sounds divine - could you please send me a recipe post haste?

Yours faithfully

T Ravenscroft (Mr)

*

MARS

Mr T Ravenscroft
17 Lingland Road
New Mills

Dear Mr Ravenscroft

Thank you for your recent letter regarding a recipe for Deep Fried MARS bars.

Although we have produced a MARS recipe book in the past we unfortunately no longer have any copies available.

We are sorry that we could not be of assistance on this occasion but would like to thank you again for the interest you have shown in writing to us.

Please accept the enclosed MARS confectionery voucher as a token of our appreciation.

Yours sincerely
Jackie Corriette, Marketing Department

*

17 Lingland Road
New Mills
CHESHIRE

28th April

Jackie Corriette
Mars Confectionary
Slough

Dear Jackie Corriette

You took so long to reply to my letter of 25th March that in the meantime impatience got the better of me and I deep-fried a Mars bar without the advantage of a recipe.

You will be pleased to learn that I managed to fry the Mars Bar in batter without too much trouble, but problems arose when I tried to eat it. My favoured way of consuming your divine confection is to cut it up into bite-size pieces, place the pieces on my wife's naked body, and then eat them off her. (She does the same thing to me but she prefers Toblerone, for some reason). It was tricky to say the least, cutting the hot gooey Mars bar into bite-size pieces, but even trickier trying to put them on my wife, the trouble being that they were still quite hot. Consequently she had great difficulty keeping still and they kept slipping off. Several pieces ended up on the bedroom floor and in the bedding, picking up fluff. Consequently I ended up with only one fluff-free piece, and even that was inedible, as by the time my wife could stand it on her body it was cold (The Mars Bar, not her body).

With the above in mind, should you ever bring out another recipe book and you include deep fried Mars Bars in it, I think you would be as well to point out that one shouldn't attempt to eat it in this manner.

Yours faithfully

T Ravenscroft (Mr)

****

17 Lingland Road
New Mills
CHESHIRE
15th April

Batchelors Foods
Croydon

Dear Batchelors Foods

I have just used one of your Delicately Flavoured Rice packets, and very nice it was too. I just wish there had been more of it. In fact I expected there to be more of it, as it clearly stated on the packet '3 to 4 servings'. To whom exactly, sparrows?

If this seems facetious it certainly isn't meant to be, because after following your cooking instructions, and dividing the cooked rice into four, I can honestly say that each of the four portions was a good deal smaller than the portions of rice I saw being doled out to the prisoners of war in the film 'The Bridge on the River Kwai'. In fact if they'd had to survive on your portions of Delicately Flavoured Rice there's a good chance they would still be building the bridge, Alec Guinness or no Alec Guinness. Is it possible that I got a faulty packet?

Yours faithfully

T Ravenscroft (Mr)

*

Batchelors

April 21,
REF 0061055A
Mr T Ravenscroft
17 Lingland Road
New Mills

Cheshire

Dear Mr Ravenscroft

We regret to learn of your recent experience with a packet of Batchelors Delicately Flavoured Rice.

We continuously monitor our quality control procedures to ensure that we achieve consistently high levels of product quality and the most meticulous care is taken to enable you to enjoy all our products in perfect condition. It is therefore particularly disappointing to us that in this instance our product failed to give you complete satisfaction.

We would stress that this product, is of course, intended as an accompaniment to a meal. Before any new products are launched by us on a national scale, they are first test marketed in one or two areas for a long period of time. In this way we are able to collect all kinds of consumer reaction to the product, the type and design of packaging and, of course, quantities, texture and taste.

We sincerely regret that despite the precautions undertaken that you have had cause to bring this matter to our attention. We wish to express our sincere apologies for the inconvenience caused from this purchase and very much hope that you will accept the reimbursement enclosed as a goodwill gesture from our part. We trust that you will find all future purchases to your satisfaction.

Yours sincerely

Jayne Pratt (Mrs)
Customer Services Manager
Enclosure(s)

4xBatchelors 50p Voucher

*

17 Lingland Road

New Mills

CHESHIRE

27th April

Jayne Pratt

Batchelors

Crawley

Dear Jayne Pratt

Reference your letter of 21st April.

I wasn't complaining about the quality of your Delicately Flavoured Rice. As I pointed out in my letter, the quality was excellent, and certainly a quantum leap better than the 'I Can't Believe It's Not Butter!' that I recently had cause to write to you about when you were wearing your Van Den Bergh Foods hat. (Are you moonlighting by the way?). No, my complaint is that you were a bit skinny with the rice. I took advantage of the vouchers you sent me and purchased with them two more packets of Delicately Flavoured Rice, the Pilau and the Garlic & Butter versions. Both were very tasty with a few oven chips, but still miserly in portion size.

It isn't for me to tell you your business of course, and I wouldn't dream of doing so, but I really do think that the 'I Can't Believe It's Not Butter' arm of your company is letting down the Batchelors side. You would do well to disassociate yourself from them.

Yours faithfully

T Ravenscroft (Mr)

****

17 Lingland Road
New Mills
CHESHIRE

16th April

Uncle Ben's
Master Foods UK
PE30 4JE

130

Dear Uncle Ben

I have just dined on a jar of your Sweet and Sour Sauce, which I had with chicken and a rather frugal, to put it mildly, portion of Batchelor's Delicately Flavoured Rice. (I should have taken the advice on your label and used Uncle Ben's Long Grain Rice instead!)

It is an irony then that it is about something on your label about which I feel I must take you to task. However, before I start beefing, I would like to make it quite clear that the taste of your Sweet and Sour Sauce is excellent, quite the best I have ever tasted outside a Chinese restaurant, and a good deal better than most of them! No, my niggle concerns your use of the words 'A sweet and sour sauce with a selection of crispy vegetables'. Now I won't deny that the vegetables in question could have been crispy at some time in their career, but they certainly weren't very crispy when they reached my bowl and chopsticks. 'Soggy' would be a more apt description of their condition. But then how could they be crispy? Let's face it, after lying in sweet and sour sauce for any length of time it would take a bamboo pole all it's time to remain crispy, never mind a bamboo shoot. I realise of course that you can't very well print 'A sweet and sour sauce with a selection of soggy vegetables' on your label, as this would no doubt put the customers off and you have to make a living, but why not dispense with the description altogether? I am sure it does little to influence the customer's choice, and it would make an honest company out of you.

Otherwise keep up the good work.

Yours faithfully

T Ravenscroft (Mr)

131

Master Foods

April 21st
Mr T Ravenscroft
17 Lingland Road
New Mills
Cheshire

Dear Mr Ravenscroft

We were most concerned to receive your letter advising us of your disappointment with your recent purchase of Uncle Ben's Sweet & Sour With Vegetables.

We take great care in the development of our products to ensure that they meet the needs of the consumer and during the manufacture of our products we insist on a high level of quality for raw materials and in-plant processing.

We introduced this product into the market after conducting product and consumer research to ensure that as responsible food manufacturers the product was acceptable to our customers.

We do take notice of what our customers have to say, and have accordingly forwarded your comments on to our Marketing and R&D colleagues for consideration. We apologise for the inconvenience this has caused, and enclose compensation which we hope will make amends for your disappointment.

Yours sincerely

MASTER FOODS

Nancy Livingstone
Customer Services

*

17 Lingland Road

New Mills

CHESHIRE

22nd April

Nancy Livingstone
Master Foods
King's Lynn

Dear Nancy Livingstone

133

You seem to have got the wrong idea entirely from my letter. I certainly wasn't disappointed with Uncle Ben's Sweet and Sour Sauce, far from it. No, the point I was making is that your 'selection of crispy vegetables' weren't crispy, but nor could they be, so why not dispense with this description and make an honest company of yourself? Remember the words of Robert Maxwell - ' An honest company is a happy company'.

I am pleased that you have passed on my comments to your Marketing and R & D colleagues, and will be most interested in what they have to say. Should I contact them direct or can I leave it to you to pass on their observations to me?

Yours faithfully

T Ravenscroft (Mr)

NO REPLY!

****

17 Lingland Road
New Mills
CHESHIRE

17th March

Hyde's Brewery
46 Moss Lane West
Manchester

Dear Hyde's Brewery

I am writing to you in my official capacity as secretary of the New Mills Invalids Club. As part of our Spring activities the club would like to visit your brewery, if Hydes do a brewery tour that is. If so, perhaps you could write to me stating prices, visiting times, discounts for invalids, etcetera.

I visualise that no more than twenty club members will be interested as that is the number which took advantage of our trip to the Black Sheep Brewery in Yorkshire last year, which was most enjoyable apart from a couple of incidents.

One thing I must be aware of before our visit is if any of your overhead walkways are made of metal diamond mesh. I ask this because at the Black Sheep Brewery one of our invalids, Mr Grimshaw, got his peg leg stuck in their overhead diamond mesh walkway, causing a half hour delay and much embarrassment, especially when the tour behind caught up with us and couldn't get past. Why Mr Grimshaw insists on wearing a peg leg when proper artificial legs are freely available nowadays I really don't know, but I suspect it's because he likes people to know he was once in the Navy. Anyway the thing is if Hydes have similar walkways I shall simply tell Mr Grimshaw that he can't come.

You need have no fears however about the rest of we invalids. Despite our afflictions we are all quite active, sound in wind if not in limb, and are able to get about (no wheelchairs) perfectly well. One of our two epileptic members caused us a bit of concern during the visit to Black Sheep when he had a fit and almost fell into a vat of fermenting hops but you can rest assured that on our visit to Hydes that I, as club secretary, will be keeping a very close watch on him.

Yours sincerely

T Ravenscroft (Mr)

*

HYDES

Mr T Ravenscroft
Lingland Road
New Mills

Dear Mr Ravenscroft

With reference to your letter dated 17th March, firstly please accept my apologies for the delay in getting back to you.

We do operate tours at Hydes brewery that are available Monday to Thursday evenings throughout the year. The tours cost £7.50 per person which includes the tour of the brewery and a complimentary bar for the evening so you will be able to sample a wide collection of beers. However I do offer a discount for some groups and I would be happy to offer you places at £6 each. Tours start at 7.30pm and last orders is rung in the bar shortly before 10.00pm. You would need to arrange a date in advance so that I can arrange an appropriate number of places for you and the easiest way to do this is to give me a call and I will talk through the availability with you. To the best of my knowledge none of our walkways are made of diamond mesh so there is little danger of Mr Grimshaw's peg leg causing any problems.

I look forward to speaking with you soon,

Kind regards

Paul Mouat
Marketing Executive, Hydes Brewery

*

17 Lingland Road
New Mills
CHESHIRE

20th April

Paul Mouatt
Hyde's Brewery

137

46 Moss Lane West
Manchester

Dear Paul Mouat

You were so tardy in replying to my letter that I thought the prospect of your having to cope with Mr Grimshaw had put you off, but apparently I have misjudged you. Even so I hope you are not so dilatory at Hydes in the manufacture of your ales or the pubs could soon run dry.

In fact, because you were so long in replying, I have in the meantime arranged a visit to Samuel Smith's Tadcaster Brewery in North Yorkshire instead. In addition to replying to my letter most promptly they couldn't have been more helpful. One of their walkways is made of diamond mesh but rather than say no to Mr Grimshaw they have arranged to cover it with plywood during our visit, so as long as Mr Grimshaw's pegleg doesn't go through the plywood everything will be hunky dory.

I am still however interested in bringing a party of invalids to Hydes, but probably in the summer now. In view of the fact that you disappointed us with our proposed spring visit would you be prepared to offer us a more generous group rate than £6.00 each? Say £4.00 each and £6.00 for the conjoined twins?

I look forward to your affirmative reply.

Yours sincerely

T Ravenscroft (Mr)

NO REPLY!

****

17 Lingland Road
New Mills
CHESHIRE

17th April

Aunt Bessie's
Tryton Foods

139

Trinity Street
Hull

Dear Aunt Bessie

I have just had the misfortune to try one of your Yorkshire Pudding Beef Dinners. I say misfortune, because what might have been an excellent meal was spoiled by the lack of adequate heating instructions on the packet. Your instructions clearly state 'Remove carton and film wrapping, leaving paper disc on meal, and place on a suitable plate'. As my wife quite rightly pointed out, at no stage in the subsequent instructions is one told to remove the paper disc.

Now you might argue that it would only be common sense to remove the paper disc once the meal is heated through, but unfortunately common sense is not a commodity which my wife has an abundance of - between you and me I married her for her looks - so consequently she served up the meal to me with the paper disc still between the Yorkshire Pudding Dinner and the plate. Eating paper, even along with a Yorkshire Pudding Dinner, is not a pleasant experience. Whether or not it was eating the paper disc which gave me diarrhoea the following day I'm not sure - if I *was* sure this letter would be coming from my solicitor, not me - but what I am quite sure of is that it was an altogether unpleasant and unnecessary experience. This can't be the first time it has happened, and to ensure that it doesn't happen again I suggest that you immediately amend the instructions on your packet accordingly.

Yours faithfully

T Ravenscroft (Mr)

Tryton Foods

Our Ref 662/JB/MG/97
23 April
Mr T Ravenscroft
17 Lingland Road
New Mills
Cheshire

Dear Mr Ravenscroft

WITHOUT PREJUDICE

Thank you for your letter of 17 April which we have read with interest. We sell approximately 250,000 units annually of Beef Dinner (and the same of Chicken Dinner) and you may be surprised to know that your letter is the first of its kind. You state in your letter that the paper was 'between the plate and the pudding', I am intrigued to know whether it was also served to you upside down as the paper covers and protects the pudding contents!

However, we are sorry to hear that the product was served to you in an uncustomary fashion, which I am sure was in no way beneficial to its eating quality.

We hope the enclosed voucher to the value of £3.00 will help persuade you that Aunt Bessie's products can indeed be most enjoyable.

Yours sincerely

Jacky Bowes
Technical Controller

*

17 Lingland Road
New Mills
CHESHIRE

28th April

Your ref 662/JB/MG/97
Jacky Bowes
Tryton Foods
Hull

Dear Jacky Bowes

Thank you for your letter of 23rd April.

I suppose on reflection that, as you have intimated, the Beef Dinner must have been served up to me upside down. This would not come as a surprise to you, nor would the fact that it is apparently the first time it has ever happened despite your selling 250,000 units annually, if you had been exposed to the culinary expertise of my wife for any length of time. We are talking here of a woman who once roasted an undrawn chicken. She had also contrived to stuff the fowl with sage and onion stuffing, though don't ask me how. I am quite confident that without too much effort she could burn water.

I hope for your sake that you have been luckier than me in your choice of wife, Jacky, although I very much doubt it, because in my experience the only time women know what they're doing is when they're on the lavatory.

With your vouchers I tried Aunt Bessie's Toad in the Hole, taking the precaution of heating it up myself. It was very nice, although I would have preferred a little more Toad and a bit less Hole. Your portion control manager didn't work for Batchelors at one time, did he?

Yours faithfully

T Ravenscroft (Mr)

A few days after I sent the preceding letter I received through the post a piece of toilet paper on which had been written 'Guess who?' As the envelope was postmarked 'Hull' I suspect that it was sent by Jacky Bowes of Aunt Bessie's. Probably for daring to criticise their Toad in the Hole.

****

17 Lingland Road
New Mills
CHESHIRE

20th April

Bird's Eye Wall's Ltd
Walton-on- Thames
Surrey
KT12 1NT

143

Dear Bird's Eye Wall's

I have long been a fan of your Boil-in-the bag Kipper Fillets and have them for breakfast every day when I am at home. However, I have to spend a good deal of my time on the Continent on business. With a little effort it is sometimes possible to buy fresh kippers whilst abroad, but I have as yet never been able to buy your Boil-in-the-bag Kipper Fillets, which I much prefer.

In an effort to simulate the taste I have tried boiling a plastic bag in the pan along with the fresh kippers, in the hope that they would take on the unique boil-in-the-bag flavour, but sadly the kippers have always remained resolutely unboiled-in-the-bag-like. With this in mind I was wondering if you could advise me on anything else I could try in my efforts to get fresh kippers to taste like yours?

I look forward to hearing from you.

Yours faithfully

T Ravenscroft (Mr)

*

Birds Eye Wall's

14 May
Mr T Ravenscroft
23Hillside View
New Mills
Cheshire

Dear Mr Ravenscroft,

Thank you for your letter about our boil-in-bag kippers. As you have discovered, we do not export these to anywhere in Europe; I think the whole concept is essentially British.

The result which you get from the Birds Eye product is not actually imparted by the plastic itself and this would account for the fact that you cannot get such a good result if you add a plastic bag to the water when you cook kippers abroad. The flavour and succulence of these kippers is largely due to the fact that they are packed into the sealed bag (together with butter pat) and then quick frozen immediately after curing. The quick freezing ensures that the fish is kept really fresh tasting, and this taste is preserved by the fact that nothing is lost in the water and steam which is involved in boiling or poaching in an open pan.

You do not say whether the kippers you buy abroad are ready frozen, but I suspect that they are not. So it is not possible from this point of view to simulate the flavour. But it is possible to buy very strong, boilable plastic bags in which you can create your own boil-in-bag dishes. You simply put the raw - frozen or unfrozen - fish or meat into the bag, adding butter or other seasoning and excluding as much air as you can, then secure the neck of the bag with a strong wire tie or a heat sealer. It can then be boiled in the normal way. But sadly even this would not guarantee that you will get the unique Birds Eye effect because obviously the quality of the fish itself is likely to be variable.

I hope this is helpful

LINDA BELL
Assistant Consumer Services Manager

17 Lingland Road
New Mills
CHESHIRE

21st May

Linda Bell
Bird's Eye Wall's Ltd
Walton-on- Thames

Dear Linda Bell

Thank you for your letter of 14th May.

I took your advice and made myself some do-it-yourself boil-in-the-bag kippers. I bought a quantity of kippers from my local fishmonger, who assured me that they were of the finest quality, put them in a strong plastic bag with a generous pat of Lurpak - I wouldn't insult them with 'I Can't Believe It's Not Butter' - excluded all the air, then sealed them with my wife's steam iron. (If I do any more I will have to think of something else, because after using the iron the following day my wife complained that her leotard smelt of fish).

I am afraid that the result was a bit of a disappointment, as the kippers did not reach your high standard. However I then tried an experiment, boiling a pair of kippers, which I had purchased at the same time, with one of your boil-in-the-bag plastic bags. These kippers tasted exactly the same as yours! It wasn't just my imagination either, because in order to test my findings I then boiled two Aunt Bessie's Individual Yorkshire Puddings, one in an ordinary plastic bag and one in one of your plastic bags, and the one boiled in your plastic bag tasted far superior.

It would appear then that your plastic bags have a greater influence on the taste of your kippers than you give them credit for. With this in mind I was wondering if I could purchase a quantity of them from you?

Yours faithfully

T Ravenscroft (Mr)

*

Birds Eye Wall's

11 June
Mr T Ravenscroft
17 Lingland Road
New Mills
Cheshire

Dear Mr Ravenscroft,

Thank you for your further letter about getting the authentic boil-in-bag taste with your kippers. I am sorry that my suggestions did not give you a satisfactory result.

I very much regret that we are not able to supply you with some of these bags. Quite apart from anything else, it would be impossible for us to donate any items of packaging, not so much because of its value but because our production plants simply do not have the human resource which would be needed to extract these items from pallets, pack them up, address and despatch them on a regular basis. But in any case the bags are not preformed; we buy the all this type of polythene packaging on a roll and the machine which packs the products also shapes and seals the bags.

I am sorry to disappoint you. I fear you will have to keep on buying the Birds Eye brand for complete satisfaction.

LINDA BELL
Assistant Consumer Services Manager

*

17 Lingland Road
New Mills
CHESHIRE
17th June

Linda Bell
Bird's Eye Wall's Ltd
Walton-on- Thames

Dear Linda Bell

Thank you for your letter of 11th June. However you don't shake off a boil-in-the-bag kipper fan as easily as that! Regarding your point about your inability to supply me on a regular basis, there would be no need for you to do this as I will quite happily take a lifetimes supply at one go. I have worked out my requirements, and, assuming that I live to be eighty (which I am sure to do if I continue to eat Bird's Eye Boil-in-the-bag Kipper Fillets!), I will need a roll of polythene 2125 metres long by one metre wide.

Fortunately I will be in the Walton-on-Thames area on the 1st of August, so I will pop into your factory to pick it up. In the meantime if you could let me know the cost I will put you a cheque in the post.

Yours faithfully
T Ravenscroft (Mr)

*

Birds Eye Wall's

07 July
Mr T Ravenscroft
17 Lingland Road
New Mills
Cheshire

Dear Mr Ravenscroft,

Thank you for your further letter on the subject of boil-in-bag kippers. I am sorry that we are not able to help you by supplying some of the material in question. We receive a number of requests for packaging - tubs, plates, saucers, foil trays and so on - but unfortunately do not have the mechanisms by which we can respond to these requests.

Incidentally, the address here at Walton-on-Thames is an office, not a factory, so there is no stock of any packaging material held here.

Please accept our apologies once again.

LINDA BELL
Assistant Consumer Services Manager

*

17 Lingland Road

New Mills
CHESHIRE

10th July

Linda Bell
Bird's Eye Wall's Ltd
Walton-on- Thames

Dear Linda Spoilsport Bell

I really expected better from a company whose products I buy at least five times a week. I will never eat Bird's Eye Boil-in-the-bag Kipper Fillets again!

Yours faithfully

T Ravenscroft (Mr)

****

17 Lingland Road
New Mills
CHESHIRE

21st April

Bernard Matthews Foods Ltd
Norwich

150

Norfolk

Dear Bernard Matthews

Very surprisingly I have a complaint to make about your Willy Whales. I say surprisingly because, although I am not personally familiar with your turkey products, preferring my turkey only at Christmas and with traditional chestnut stuffing and oven chips, my three children absolutely love them.

The complaint comes from my middle son Henry, who says that your Willy Whales taste fishy. Now it must be admitted that Henry has not the most discerning of palates, far too much junk food passes his lips for him to be able to claim that, but I tried a bite of a Willy Whale myself and I must say I agree with him.

I realise of course that your turkeys are fed fish products, and that this can lead to your turkey meat usually tasting a bit of the fishy side, but in particular the turkey meat in your Willy Whales was extremely fishy to say the least. Maybe you could offer up an explanation for this?

Yours faithfully

T Ravenscroft (Mr)

*

Bernard Matthews

Mr T Ravenscroft
17 Lingland Road
New Mills
Cheshire

Dear Mr Ravenscroft,

Thank you for your letter concerning a pack of Willy Whales you recently purchased. We are indeed sorry that it was necessary for you to contact us and we are pleased to be given the opportunity to resolve the matter.

Willy Whales are one of the products from our fish range and as the packaging states are 'crunchy golden whale shapes made from selected flaked white fish'. However, if your son was expecting a turkey product, we can appreciate his concern.

In the circumstances we have pleasure in enclosing our cheque for £10.00 and we feel certain you will receive every satisfaction from our products in the future.

Yours sincerely, for
BERNARD MATTHEWS FOODS LTD.

Anne Peters

*

17 Lingland Road
New Mills
CHESHIRE

15th May

Your ref BM9710099-1

152

Anne Peters
Bernard Matthews Foods Ltd
Norwich

Dear Anne Peters

Thank you for your letter of 7th May, and the cheque for £10.00. At first I was going to return it, as I don't normally accept charity. However on this occasion I decided to keep it as compensation for a bad experience I had the only time I ever tried one of your Lamb Roasts.

Turning to the matter of your Willy Whales it would seem that I owe you an apology. My wife has since bought another packet and you are quite correct, the packet does state that they are 'crunchy golden whale shapes'. I must say I feel you are being a bit ambitious in likening them to a whale though, because if Willy Whales are indeed whale-shaped then the whale in question belongs to a species of whale that I certainly have never come across. In fact to my eyes your Willy Whales are just as likely to be taken for willies as they are for whales.

It is quite amazing how one's opinion can change once in possession of all the facts, isn't it. Before I received your letter I thought that Willy Whales were turkey pieces that tasted a bit like fish. Now I know they are made of fish however my perception of them is completely different, because I can categorically say that they are fish pieces that taste a bit like turkey. Do you think this could be because you deep-fry them in the same fat in which you fry your turkey products?

Yours faithfully

T Ravenscroft (Mr)

153

NO REPLY!

****

17 Lingland Road
New Mills
CHESHIRE

Bisto Foods
Middlewich
Cheshire

154

Dear Bisto Foods

Last week my wife inadvertently put a pair of my middle son Henry's trousers into a bucket of water to soak, prior to washing them. It later transpired that there was a packet of your Bisto Gravy Granules in one of the pockets. Unfortunately there were also six pairs of my white underpants in the bucket, and, after being soaked overnight, they became brown underpants. (Why on earth my wife finds it necessary to soak my underpants prior to washing them is a mystery that only she knows the answer to). However, after being put through the washer my underpants more or less reverted back to white, but had taken on a distinct smell of gravy. Now I quite like the smell of gravy, but not on my underpants, and yesterday on my walk from the railway station a dog followed me all the way home.

The thing is, I'm sure that your workers clothes must become permeated with the smell of Bisto Gravy Granules and take on the similar 'Bisto Gravy' smell of my underpants, so I was wondering if you could ask them how they get rid of the smell, and let me know?

Yours faithfully

T Ravenscroft (Mr)

*

BISTO FOODS

21st May
Mr T Ravenscroft
17 Lingland Road
New Mills

155

Cheshire

Dear Mr Ravenscroft,

Thank you for your recent letter regarding an enquiry about our product Bisto Gravy Granules. We were most interested in your letter due to the unusual nature of the information you required.

We have enquired with the industrial laundry that launder our protective workwear and they have assured us that normal domestic washing soap or detergents and washing machines will remove any of the food flavours and colours used in our products.

Yours sincerely,
J K HANSON
CONSUMER SERVICES

*

17 Lingland Road
New Mills
CHESHIRE

27th May

J K Hanson

156

Bisto Foods
Middlewich
Cheshire

Dear J K Hanson

Since writing to you on 25th April something quite remarkable has happened. It's rather personal, so I would appreciate it if you would keep it to yourself. The thing is, the day after writing to you my wife and I made love, it being Saturday, after Match of the Day. My wife although very appreciative, has up to now always been a silent lover, but her beauty more than makes up for her lack of vocal enthusiasm. However on this occasion, and but a few seconds into the act, she emitted a quite loud and appreciative "Aaaaaah." This of course pleased me immensely. My joy was short-lived however, because almost immediately afterwards she followed the "Aaaaaah" with a cry of "Bisto!"

What had apparently happened was that she had caught a whiff of my Bisto-impregnated underpants. Initially I was a little put out to say the least, what with my efforts at love-making coming second in the appreciation stakes to a jar of gravy granules, but we carried on and it turned out to be the most satisfying bout of sex we have had in our entire married life.

Since then I have worn Bisto-flavoured underpants to bed every night, and our sex life has been utterly transformed. Rather than try to remove the smell of Bisto from my underpants I now ensure that they are always given a good soaking in 'Bisto water' prior to being washed. (Despite what you say in your letter about normal domestic washing soap removing the smell, it does tend to linger).

Why the smell of Bisto turns my wife on I neither know nor care. Maybe it is the 'animal' smell of it. I would be interested to know if you have ever come across this sort of thing before, as I am considering using it as the subject of a speech I will soon be giving to the New Mills Young Mothers Group.

Yours faithfully

T Ravenscroft (Mr)

NO REPLY!

****

17 Lingland Road
New Mills
CHESHIRE

26th April

G Costa and Co Ltd
Aylesford
ME20 7NA

Dear G Costa

My wife is forever making disparaging remarks about my breath and pointedly leaving Clorets round the house, so you can imagine my delight when I read on a can of your Blue Dragon Water Chestnuts that they 'are considered 'yin', and cooling, and are thought to sweeten the breath'. Here we go, I said to myself, cool sweet breath, just the thing to quieten her. So the following day I stir-fried the whole of the contents of the can with some diced squid, about half-a-dozen cloves of garlic, four slices of root ginger, and a dessertspoonful of five spice powder, and ate the lot with some Bachelors Aromatic Rice. Then, confident in the knowledge that my breath would pass muster, I walked up to my wife and planted a smacker full on her lips. She kicked me! At a loss as to her behaviour, I asked her why. She told me that I smelled like a drain.

In view of the claim on your can that my breath would be cool and sweet after eating your water chestnuts, would you care to explain this?

Yours faithfully

T Ravenscroft (Mr)

*

G COSTA

Ref: JD
Mr T Ravenscroft
17 Lingland Road
New Mills

Cheshire

Dear Mr Ravenscroft,

Re: Blue Dragon Water Chestnuts

Thank you for your letter of 26th April regarding our Blue Dragon Water Chestnuts.

We appreciate your comments regarding the breath freshening aspect of this vegetable, however, as with any food if it is mixed with other ingredients, especially those with strong flavour such as garlic, unfortunately the effect is not the same!

We have also scoured our stock to locate a label claiming these freshening qualities.

Thank you for purchasing Blue Dragon.

Yours sincerely, for G COSTA & CO LTD

Joanne Dann, Consumer Relations Department

*

17 Lingland Road
New Mills
CHESHIRE

15th May

Your ref JD

Joanne Dann
G Costa and Co Ltd
Aylesford
Kent

Dear Joanne Dann

If you have in fact scoured your stock to locate on the label the claim that your Blue Dragon Water Chestnuts have freshening qualities then all I can say is you need a new scourer.

I attach, for your information, a label which clearly claims such qualities, and I consider that if you make such claims you should be prepared to stand by them. Furthermore, your failing to point out on your label that if your water chestnuts are mixed with other ingredients then their power to sweeten their breath is negated, which resulted in my suffering a badly bruised shin, is nothing less than negligence. Unless you want to risk others meeting the same fate I would seriously consider a major label rethink if I were you. I had to buy another can of your water chestnuts in order to obtain a label so I expect you to reimburse me with the cost.

Yours faithfully

T Ravenscroft (Mr)

*

G COSTA

Ref: JD
22nd May
Mr T Ravenscroft
161

17 Lingland Road
New Mills
Cheshire

Dear Mr Ravenscroft,

Re: Blue Dragon Water Chestnuts

Thank you for your letter of 15th May regarding the above. I appreciate your comments regarding our labelling. I can confirm that the new labels are indeed not quite the same as the one you have supplied to us.

As requested, please find enclosed a postal order for £1.00 in respect of the tin of Water Chestnuts purchased for its label.

Thank you for purchasing Blue Dragon.

Yours sincerely, for G COSTA & CO LTD

Joanne Dann, Consumer Relations Department

*

17 Lingland Road
New Mills
CHESHIRE

28th May

Joanne Dann
G Costa and Co Ltd
Aylesford
Kent

Dear Joanne Dann

Thank you for your letter of 22nd May.

I have visited several supermarkets and scoured the labels of your Blue Dragon Water Chestnuts but have found no evidence whatsoever of any change in the wording on them. I have also scoured the envelope of your letter and found no evidence of a £1.00 postal order! Perhaps the inefficient employee who scoured your stock for evidence of your claiming freshening qualities for your water chestnuts was the same person who was responsible for putting the postal order in the envelope?

Would you now be good enough to send me one of your new labels, so that I can check if the new wording is satisfactory, along with a postal order for £1.30 to cover the postal order that you claim to have already sent but haven't, plus the 30 pence it is going to cost me to send this additional letter.

Yours faithfully

T Ravenscroft (Mr)

*

G COSTA

Ref: JD
11 June
Mr T Ravenscroft
163

17 Lingland Road
New Mills
Cheshire

Dear Mr Ravenscroft,

Re: Blue Dragon Water Chestnuts

We acknowledge receipt of your recent letter dated 28 May and apologise that the Postal Order was omitted from our letter of 22 May.

Accordingly we enclose a Postal Order for £2.00 and trust you will find this satisfactory.

Yours sincerely, for G COSTA & CO LTD

Elizabeth Sims
Consumer Relations Department

****

17 Lingland Road
New Mills
CHESHIRE

27th April

Taylors of Harrogate
Yorkshire Tea
Harrogate
North Yorkshire

Dear Taylors of Harrogate

Although I have always lived quite close to Yorkshire I must confess that I have never felt the desire to visit the White Rose county. Maybe this is because the names of some of the towns and villages sound so uninviting - Greaseborough, Slaithwaite and Grewelthorpe spring readily to mind, but no doubt I could find a Snotborough if I tried hard enough. Probably by the time God got to Yorkshire He must have run out of attractive names and you got the barrel-scrapings, as it were. However, and to get to the point, I have recently been introduced to the delights of 'Yorkshire Tea', which in turn has led to me to deciding to visit your county in the not too distant future. If the climate in Yorkshire is hot enough to grow tea then clearly I have been missing something! During my stay I would like very much to visit your tea plantations. Would this be possible?

I look forward to hearing from you.

Yours faithfully

T Ravenscroft (Mr)

*

TAYLORS of HARROGATE

Dear Mr Ravenscroft

Thank you for your recent letter and kind comments about Yorkshire Tea. We always enjoy reading the letters from our Yorkshire Tea customers and we really do appreciate the time and trouble taken to write. We were particularly delighted to read that you were thinking of visiting Yorkshire for the first time thanks to your enjoyment of our tea!

We are still a small family business with over a hundred year's experience of buying and blending tea. Our Tea Buyer visits tea estates around the world, selecting only the very best tea for our blends. This helps to give Yorkshire Tea its rich refreshing flavour. However it does mean that you would have to travel much further afield than Yorkshire to visit tea plantations.

Thank you once again for your letter and your interest in our business. Please find enclosed a sample of Yorkshire Tea so that you can enjoy your next cup with our compliments.

Yours sincerely

Katy Squire
Assistant PR & Promotions Manager

*

17 Lingland Road
New Mills
Cheshire

Katy Squire
Taylors of Harrogate
Harrogate
North Yorkshire

Dear Katy Squire

Thank you for your letter of 1st May and the sample of Yorkshire Tea. I used it to make a pot of tea, which I shared with the vicar when he called round to bless my eldest son Marcus's new iguana, and he was converted. (To Yorkshire tea, that is, he was already converted to the Church of England faith, naturally)

I was both surprised and disappointed to learn that the tea that goes into Yorkshire tea isn't grown in Yorkshire. It's none of my business, I will be the first to admit, but aren't you breaking the Trades Description Act or something by calling it Yorkshire Tea?

Yours faithfully

T Ravenscroft (Mr)

*

TAYLORS of HARROGATE

8th May

Dear Mr Ravenscroft

Thank you for your recent letter. We were delighted to read that you have converted your Vicar to Yorkshire Tea! Thank you also for your enquiry regarding the name of Yorkshire Tea. We would love to be able to grow tea here in Harrogate although sadly the climatic conditions are far from ideal! Instead our Tea Buyer visits tea estates and tea gardens around the world searching for fine quality teas to use in our blends.

Taylors of Harrogate was founded in 1886 and we remain very proud of our Yorkshire heritage. Still today all our teas are blended and packed in Harrogate and for this reason our rich, refreshing blend is called Yorkshire Tea. The name is registered and trademarked.

Thank you once again for your interest in our business and we do hope you will continue to enjoy drinking Yorkshire Tea.

Yours sincerely

Katy Squire, Assistant PR & Promotions Manager

*

17 Lingland Road
New Mills
CHESHIRE

Katy Squire
Taylors of Harrogate
Harrogate
North Yorkshire

Dear Katy Squire

Hello again! Just a line to let you know that last weekend my wife and I visited the Yorkshire Dales, staying in Wharfedale. What a lovely part of the country! And such very nice people. The only disappointment apart from the unseasonable weather was with the Yorkshire Tea, which we drank whilst in Yorkshire. For some reason it didn't taste nearly so good as it does here in Derbyshire. As a matter of fact it wasn't all that easy to come by either, and I had to get the landlady at the guest house where we were staying to buy in some Yorkshire Tea specially, as she 'Allus got that tea what t' monkeys advertises on t' telly as it were a seet bloody tastier', as she put it most charmingly. I wonder if this could have something to do with the water?

I ask this because the domestic water supply in the Cheshire is excellent, and far superior to the water that emerged through our tap in Grassington. In fact my wife refused point blank to drink Grassington tap water and I had to go all the way to Skipton to get her a bottle of Perrier, but then she's always been a bit squeamish about what she will put into her mouth ever since our honeymoon (when she got drunk on Cherry B).

You remember the vicar I introduced to Yorkshire Tea? The other day he ran off with a lady bell ringer, but I doubt it was anything to do with drinking your tea.

169

Yours faithfully

T Ravenscroft (Mr)

****

17 Lingland Road
New Mills
CHESHIRE

HP Foods

170

Tower Road
Birmingham

Dear H P Foods

Being something of a gourmet I make a point of watching as
many television cookery programmes as my time will permit.
However despite seeing all that the Two Fat Ladies have to offer,
and sitting through Rick Stein, Gary Rhodes, Raymond Blanc, the
Roux Brothers, countless series of Delia Smith, and Floyd on
France, Italy, Spain, Australia and God knows where else, I have
yet to see a single TV chef use HP Sauce, whether included in the
recipe or on the finished dish. I find this quite amazing, as a
generous helping of your excellent condiment will improve any
dish beyond recognition. I have found that two to three
tablespoonfuls added to the boiling water absolutely transforms
Bachelors Delicately Flavoured Rice, whilst to pour it liberally
over Birds Eye Boil-In-The-Bag Kipper Fillets elevates an already
outstanding dish into food fit for a King. And what would my
Christmas dinner be like without it?

I wonder then why it is that TV Chefs seem reluctant to use it.
Could it be jealousy on their part, and that they don't like to
admit that a healthy dollop of HP Sauce would improve even
their finest efforts.

Yours faithfully

T Ravenscroft (Mr)

*

HP FOODS

Mr Ravenscroft
17 Lingland Road

New Mills
Cheshire

Dear Mr Ravenscroft

Thank you very much for your recent letter inquiring about using our product on National TV.

I have passed your letter onto our Marketing Department for their comments. We do realise that products are used in demonstrations and in standard contracts however, the presenter is under contract not to allow the brand name to be shown. These can be tailored to Company needs apparently. You never know we may be on the big screen soon!!

I do hope the above has clarified the situation for you but should you have any further queries please do not hesitate to contact us. It is always pleasant to receive comments from valued customers, such as yourself, and we thank you for taking the time to write. From your letter you appear to thoroughly enjoy our products and use them in a variety ways. Please find enclosed a product voucher to enable you to sample and enjoy some of our other brands as Lea & Perrins Worcester Sauce, Amoy and Rajah with the same delight.

Yours sincerely

Jean James, Research and Development Administrator

*

17 Lingland Road
New Mills
CHESHIRE

15th May

Jean James
H P Foods
Tower Road
Birmingham

Dear Jean James

Sorry, I appear to have made a mistake, it isn't HP Sauce I like, it's Heinz. However with the £5 voucher you kindly sent me I bought a bottle of your sauce, and whilst not reaching the heights to which Heinz achieve it is nonetheless very, very good, especially when a soupcon of it is added to a pot of Yorkshire Tea. If Heinz ever let their quality slip, which it appears they might well be doing if their Thomas the Tank Engine and Friends Pasta Shapes are anything to go by, I shall know where to turn. Thank you.

Yours faithfully

T Ravenscroft (Mr)

****

17 Lingland Road
New Mills
CHESHIRE

English Provender Company

173

PO Box 5
Henley-on-Thames
R99 3PM

Dear English Provender

My youngest son Oscar is extremely hyperactive, and short of tying him up the only way to stop him running riot is by strictly controlling his diet. However this is only partially successful, and I am constantly on the lookout for additional means of slowing the little tyke down, short of amputation. It was with great expectations then that I tried him on your Provender Very Lazy Garlic. What a disappointment! Your product didn't make him any lazier at all, let alone very lazy. In fact after I'd made him eat six slices of toast spread thickly with it, not only did it make him even more lively than usual but he proceeded to scream the house down, and it couldn't have been the toast that was to blame because I'd made sure the bread I used was gluten-free.

I think I deserve an explanation of why your product is clearly failing to do what you claim that
it does.

Yours faithfully

T Ravenscroft (Mr)

NO REPLY!

****

17 Lingland Road
New Mills
CHESHIRE

Tendercut Meats
Eastleigh
Birchfield Lane
Hants

Dear Tendercut Meats

The other day I took a chance and purchased a packet of your frozen Tendercut Rich Meat Gravy with Sliced Leg of Lamb. As a consequence of this I wish to make a complaint about the photograph on the front of the packet. I have no complaint about the food inside, which was as expected - bland, fatty, gristly, with thick lumpy gravy. The only observation I will make is that if the meat in question came from the limb of a lamb it must have been one which had an artificial leg. It did however have the virtue of being inexpensive, and if you shop at Aldi I suppose you can't expect the quality afforded by Fortnum and Masons. No, as I say, what I wish to complain about is not the food but the picture on the packet, which is of a plateful of succulent-looking lamb slices in a most nourishing looking gravy, and bears about as much resemblance to the contents inside as does the Queen to Kevin in Coronation Street when he had a moustache.

I would appreciate your comments on this deception.

Yours faithfully
T Ravenscroft (Mr)

*

TENDERCUT MEATS

3 February
Mr Ravenscroft
175

17 Lingland Road
New Mills
Cheshire

Dear Mr Ravenscroft

Thank you for your recent letter concerning a purchase of our sliced lamb in gravy.

We have always been proud of the fact that Tendercut Meats have set the highest quality standards. With this in mind, please accept our thanks for taking the trouble to contact us with your views and comments. They help us to continue to look at ways of ensuring that each and every one of our products reaches our customers in the best possible condition.

Our product is in fact produced with New Zealand Lamb with only the leg bone and the majority of fat removed. We are delighted to inform you that within the next two months you will be able to purchase the Tendercut range of Ready Carved Joints with a new recipe; having removed E621 and E262 making the range 100% natural.

As you said, your main complaint was with the picture on the box. We are bound by law to only show a photograph that gives a true representation of the contents; in this case slices of meat in gravy, we also work very closely with trading standards when we produce all our packaging and products. However, we sincerely regret that you felt mislead and would ask you to accept the enclosed goodwill gesture. We hope this unfortunate incident has not deterred you from purchasing further products from the Tendercut range.

Yours sincerely

176

J Moule

17 Lingland Road
New Mills
CHESHIRE

J Moule
Tendercut Meats
Brickfield Lane
Eastleigh

Dear J Moule

Thank you for your letter of 3rd February, and the P.O. for £5. I will save it until such time as you bring out the Tendercut range of Ready Carved Joints with their E 621 and E262 elements removed. It is always good to hear of E numbers being got shot of, and there is an excellent chance that their removal will bring about a substantial improvement. More power to your elbow. Incidentally, what exactly are E621 and E 262 as I think one of them recently made me poorly?

Yours faithfully

T Ravenscroft (Mr)

NO REPLY!

****

17 Lingland Road
New Mills
CHESHIRE

25th March

Pork Farms
Trowbridge
Wiltshire

Dear Pork Farms

A couple of friends and I have just won a racehorse in a raffle. We have to find a name for it and as we are all fans of your pies we thought we would call it Pork Farms Pork Pies. Have you any objection to this? I don't think there's much chance of it ever winning as someone I know in the horseracing game says that from the look of it if we entered it in the three-o-clock race there would be no more than an outside chance of it being placed in the three-thirty. However I thought I'd better mention that in case you feel that a horse called Pork Farms Pork Pies coming in last might reflect badly on your pies.

Looking forward to hearing from you, with your blessing.

Yours faithfully

T Ravenscroft (Mr)

*

PORK FARMS BOWYERS

Mr Ravenscroft
17 Lingland Road
New Mills
178

Cheshire

Ref: Gj201/JJ
14 April

Dear Mr Ravenscroft

Firstly, may I apologise for the delay in responding to your letter, and secondly can I congratulate you on your recent good fortune. I must add that in my time at Pork Farms I have received some very unusual requests, but this is far and away the most unusual to date.

I am very pleased that both you and your friends are fans of our Pies, so much so that you would name your proud possession after them. However, (and here is the boring legal bit), we cannot allow any use of the Pork Farms brand name outside of our corporate control. We would need to enter a licensing agreement that would need every aspect of your hobby being agreed to and signed off by our lawyers. I think you will agree that this would be a mutually tiring affair, particularly as the object of this exercise is fun. The more generic title of Pork Pie would, of course, be entirely down to yourselves.

I apologise for this slightly bureaucratic response, but we do need to ensure that the brand name is managed correctly. I will, however, look out for Pork Pie running in the 2.30 at Kempton and, despite your reservations about the horse's talents, have a small flutter.

Please find enclosed some vouchers that will hopefully please you all (even your equine friend)!!

Regards,

Gary Johnston

*

17 Lingland Road
New Mills
CHESHIRE

25th April

Gary Johnston
Pork Farms Bowyers
Queens Drive
Nottingham

Dear Gary Johnston

Thank you for your letter of 14th April and the vouchers, although I really do wish you hadn't put the idea into my head of feeding your pork pies to our horse. The thing is, with the vouchers I bought eight pork pies, ate one of them myself - delicious, as usual - and fed the other seven to the horse. The following day it dropped dead. The vet said it could very well have been the pork pies that caused the horse to go into the violent spasms that led to it having a heart attack, and that I was 'bloody stupid'. I must say his reasoning that eating seven pork pies can cause a heart attack is totally beyond me - I've eaten four of them many a time and the horse was twice as big as me, so if you ask me it is the vet who is bloody stupid! Anyway I thought I'd better mention it to you so that you won't advise anybody else to feed pork pies to their racehorses.

On a more pleasurable note, having now owned a racehorse, my friends and I have really got the horseracing bug, so we're going to buy another one. I have checked with Tattersall's and it seems that there already is a horse called Pork Pies. (So great minds apparently *do* think alike!) So we have decided to call our new horse Not As Good As Pork Farm Pork Pies, which will fulfil the dual purpose of giving your firm a bit of a leg up, whilst not using your brand name.

Would this be acceptable to you?

Yours faithfully

T Ravenscroft (Mr)

NO REPLY!

****

17 Lingland Road
New Mills
CHESHIRE

21st February

Jordans
Consumer Care Team
Freepost BF 304
Biggleswade

Dear Jordans Porridge Oats

For the last three months I have been breakfasting each morning on a bowl of your porridge oats as part of the G I (Glycaemic Index) diet, and very good they are too. They really fill me up and set me up for the day. This alone would make them well worth the price, but I have discovered to my great joy that your oats bring with them an added benefit, and a most welcome benefit at that!

I wouldn't like this to get around of course - although I wouldn't object to you showing this letter around the office - but since starting to eat your oats my sex life has improved no end. I suppose this is in part due to my being quite a lot slimmer and thus more attractive to my wife, having lost three stones since I started the diet (I am now down to a quite presentable nineteen stones), but I'm sure that my extra energy and staying power, fuelled as it is by your oats, has played an even bigger part.

I know from personal experience that regular helpings of milk-soaked anchovies can do wonders for a chap's sex drive but I never suspected that porridge oats might do the same. Have any other of your customers experienced this phenomenon?

Yours sincerely

T Ravenscroft (Mr)

*

JORDANS

Mr T Ravenscroft
Lingland Road
New Mills
Cheshire

5 March   Ref: 2007014580

Dear Mr Ravenscroft

Thank you for your very nice letter regarding out Conservation Grade Porridge Oats. It is so pleasant to receive comments as we do try to maintain the highest standards of quality and value.

We do certainly listen to what our customers have to say and quite often changes in formulation take place because of popular opinion, although I don't think we will be putting your 'newly found extra benefit' down on the pack as a unique selling point for our porridge oats but please be assured that I will be passing copies of your letter over to our Technical and Marketing Dept, who always appreciate feedback from our customers especially when they are as positive as yours.

Thank you again for taking the time to contact us and for your support of Jordans.

Yours sincerely

Rita Farmer
<u>Consumer Advisor</u>

*

17 Lingland Road
New Mills
CHESHIRE

8th March

Rita Farmer
Consumer Adviser
W Jordan (Cereals) Ltd
Biggleswade

Dear Rita Farmer

Thank you for your prompt and courteous reply.

Despite what you say about not putting my 'newly found extra benefit' on your packet as a unique selling point for your porridge oats I must say I think you are wasting a golden opportunity. However I believe you may very well change your mind when you hear about the most wonderful slogan I have managed to come up with to promote your company's product. Wait for it .... *'Get your oats with Jordan's Oats'*. Such a witty catchphrase is guaranteed to sell thousands of extra packets, I am quite sure. What do you think?

Unfortunately I can't claim credit for the ditty as it was dreamed up by my friend Atkins down the road, who incidentally is now also a fan of your oats since I put him on to them a couple of weeks ago. Regarding Atkins I must point out that, unlike me, he has not noticed any change in his sex life since breakfasting *a la Jordan's*, but that isn't surprising as he claims to be a five nights a week and twice on Sunday man even when oat unaided, which isn't bad for a man in his early sixties, I'm sure you will agree.

One further point. I notice you claim that your packets of oats may contain wheat, barley, rye, nuts, and sesame seeds. I must say I'd never noticed any of these ingredients in your porridge so I decided to investigate further. To my great surprise, and despite going through several packets with a fine toothcomb, I found not a single trace of any of wheat, barley, rye, nuts, or sesame seeds. It is no business of mine of course but I do feel that if you are claiming your oats contain any or all of these ingredients you should make a greater effort to include them.

However this appears to be the only blot on an otherwise quite excellent copybook.

Yours sincerely

T Ravenscroft (Mr)

*

JORDANS

Mr T Ravenscroft
Lingland Road
New Mills
Cheshire

Dear Mr Ravenscroft

Thank you for your recent letter regarding our Conservation Grade Porridge Oats. Your slogan is very good but if we put claims like you suggest on our porridge oat packaging we will need to back them up with hard facts and as you are the only customer who has informed us of this precise benefit I don't think our legal department will let us get away with it. If we have a customer who was relying on this particular benefit and it did not happen for him/her we could be sued - with the litigation society we live in these days.

The point you made about the 'May contain' statement on our packaging. This is yet another incident of our marketing department thinking they are more open and informative to our customers, and all they have done is cause confusion and distress to customers. The statement is just to let customers who are severely allergic to these allergens know that they are on our site as they go into products other than the specific product they have purchased. I think your friend Atkins is quite a man, if his claims are true and if they can be proved to come with no artificial aids!!!!!! Thank you for your letters and your support of Jordans.

Rita Farmer
Consumer Advisor

*

17 Lingland Road
New Mills
CHESHIRE
20th March

Rita Farmer
Consumer Adviser
W Jordan (Cereals) Ltd

Biggleswade

Dear Rita Farmer

Thank you for your letter clearing up the 'may contain' business. I'm glad I'm not the only satisfied customer that your Marketing Department has confused. Marketing people, eh? Almost as bad as social workers in my opinion.

Regarding my friend Atkins. I showed him your letter and he assured me that he has never used any artificial aids whatsoever, apart from the time his wife went to Australia for six weeks some years ago, when he sent away to a sex shop for a 'Wankey-Doodle-Dandy', which he used for five of the six weeks. It would have been six but for some reason the contraption broke after five weeks, probably through overuse if I know Atkins.

Regarding my slogan. Yesterday afternoon I stationed myself in Tescos breakfast cereal aisle for a couple of hours (I haven't much else to do as I'm retired) and asked every person who purchased a packet of your oats the following question: 'If you are following the GI Diet has your sex life improved since you started eating Jordan's Porridge Oats?' All of them answered my question, apart from two people who for some strange reason just looked at me with their mouths agape before wandering off, and a woman who slapped my face. Twelve of the hundred or so people I asked said they were on the GI Diet (8 women, 4 men). Seven of them (3 women, 4 men) thought that it had improved their sex life, 2 vastly. I would have stayed longer and questioned more of Tescos very obliging customers but unfortunately at that stage the manager asked me to move on, possibly because the women who slapped my face had complained to him.

It would seem then that you have a very strong case for including my slogan on your packet and in your advertising. Please feel free to do so. I took the names and addresses of the seven lucky people and if you would like me to pass them on to you so that they can confirm my findings just say the word.

Yours sincerely

T Ravenscroft (Mr)

NO REPLY!

****

17 Lingland Road
New Mills
CHESHIRE

15th March

Wm Morrison Supermarkets PLC

Dear Morrison's

I am a sixty-eight-year old man and I have been buying all the family's food from your supermarket for the last twenty years. Naturally for a man of my years I am not as fit as I used to be, nor would like to be. I don't want to bore you with my illnesses, and I don't really like talking about them, but if this letter is to fulfil its purpose, which I hope it will, I have no alternative.

In fact I suffer from a hiatus hernia, a normal hernia (which thankfully I am going into hospital next month to have repaired), a trapped nerve in my spine which cause a little numbness in my arm, athlete's foot (just one foot), sciatica, arthritis, trouble with my prostate gland and anal pain.

The anal pain is by far the worst of my afflictions. I've tried everything possible to cure it, believe me; conventional medicine, acupuncture, homeopathy, hypnotherapy, aromatherapy, all to no avail. I even tried, in absolute desperation, going to a faith healer, a travelling evangelist. At the meeting the evangelist laid hands on a man's lips and partially cured his stutter, then he laid hands on a woman's chronic bad back with an equally miraculous result, but did nothing at all for my bottom when he laid hands on it. I noted however that the evangelist didn't spend anything like so much time with his hands on my bottom as he had on the other lips and leg of the other two, so that maybe had something to do with it. I would have demanded my money back but it was free, so I had to content myself with putting nothing in the collection box and taking a pound out of it, to compensate me for the disappointment. But enough of my troubles.

The thing is I've read a lot in the papers recently about the benefits of organic food - you are what you eat and all that - and having noted that you have now started stocking a large range of the same. I was wondering if you think it might benefit me health wise if I switch from Morrison's normal food to Morrison's organic food. (Not of course that I in any way blame your food for my various complaints; in fact I got my hiatus hernia at Safeways when I used to shop there).

Yours sincerely

T Ravenscroft (Mr)

*

MORRISONS SUPERMARKETS

Mr T Ravenscroft
Lingland Road
New Mills
Cheshire

Dear Mr Ravenscroft

Thank you for your letter to this department.

We always welcome feedback from our customers and assure you that your comments have been duly noted. I have taken the liberty of passing these onto the people concerned in order that they may be looked into and, if necessary, be addressed.

We pride ourselves on the high quality of products that we sell and it is always very regrettable when these do not meet our customers' requirements. You can certainly rest assure that your comments and views are very valuable to us and we will continue to do everything that to ensure that we maintain the high standards that our customers expect.

Thank you once again for taking the time to share your views with us and I very much hope that we will remain your choice for shopping in the future.

Yours sincerely

Carol Paley
Customer Services Advisor

*

17 Lingland Road
New Mills
CHESHIRE

15th March

Wm Morrison Supermarkets PLC

Dear Carol Paley.

What's going on with you at Morrison's? I sent you the attached letter and you replied to it with what seems to be the standard reply to a letter of complaint. Kindly sort yourself out and reply to my original letter would you?

Yours sincerely

T Ravenscroft (Mr)

*

MORRISONS SUPERMARKETS

Mr T Ravenscroft
17 Lingland Road
New Mills
Cheshire

Dear Mr Ravenscroft

Thank you for your letter to this department. I am sorry that you are disappointed with the response that you have received in connection with your complaint.

Our aim is to offer outstanding value for money and we firmly believe that all customers should have access to safe, wholesome, affordable food, according to their own individual tastes and preferences. We believe we have a good range of organic foods, both own label and brands, that includes, breads, dairy products, eggs, fresh fruit and vegetables, cereals, wine, tea and coffee, and other grocery items, which we feel reflects the current demands of the majority of our shoppers.

However, in relation to your question, I'm afraid that we are unable to offer any advice of Organic food will help your medical condition. We would advise you to seek advice from your GP.

Thank you once again for taking time to bring the matter to our attention and I do hope that we will remain your choice for shopping in the future.

Yours sincerely
Carol Paley
Customer Services Advisor

*

17 Lingland Road
New Mills
CHESHIRE

15th March

Wm Morrison Supermarkets PLC

Dear Carol Paley

You need have no fears that Morrison's will not remain my choice for shopping, not just in the future but for ever more! In the six weeks since I wrote to you, five of which I have been eating solely from your range of organic foods, my health has improved by leaps and bounds. While it is true to say that I haven't noticed any improvement with my bottom - in fact things have got a little worse in that department as I am breaking wind much more often than I used to - the organic broccoli probably - there has been a marked improvement in the state of my hiatus

193

hernia, my sciatica and especially my athlete's foot, which has almost cleared up completely.

However the best news is that my sex life has also improved, although this might have something to do with Jordan's Porridge Oats, which are also organic of course. In fact I am so delighted that I have had a tee shirt made with 'Morrison's Organic Food Is Simply Orgasmic' printed on the front (I am getting to be pretty nifty at slogan writing even if I say so myself). On the only time I have worn the tee shirt at Morrison's thus far it created quite a stir. Even the manager came out onto the shop floor to have a look at me, although it wasn't long before he was back in his office, but then he's a busy man I suppose.

It was my intention just to wear the tee shirt when I am doing the weekly shop at Morrison's but it occurred to me that I would be doing you a favour if I were to also wear it on the odd occasion I go to Tesco and Asda. In fact if you like, as a small repayment for the huge debt I owe you, I would be quite happy to visit both of these supermarkets now and then and just walk around for a bit without buying anything; I don't think they can stop you. Would you like me to do this? It would be no trouble.

T Ravenscroft (Mr)

NO REPLY!

Lingland Road
New Mills
CHESHIRE

23rd March

Knorr
194

Freepost ADM 3940
London

Dear Knorr

I am afraid I have a complaint to make about your Ragu Tomato and Cheese Sauce. My wife was away for the day and I was busy so I had our Norwegian au pair Anni prepare a pasta dish for the children's supper. To be quite honest Anni's culinary skills are non-existent so I only let her loose in the kitchen in emergencies, and she doesn't speak very good English either, however to make up for this she is very pretty and *very* accommodating.

What happened apparently is that Anni followed the directions on your packet a little too literally. Things went all right at first; she tipped the contents of the pouch gently into a saucepan and stirred often. It was when she carried out your serving suggestion 'for a tasty alternative throw in a small can of tuna and a handful of peas' that things went pear-shaped. For that's what Anni did, to the letter. She threw in a small can of tuna. Unopened. She didn't get round to throwing in the handful of peas because the force with which she threw in the tin of tuna caused the saucepan to fly off the hob and deposit the Ragu Cheese and Tomato Sauce on the floor.

I didn't witness the incident myself but my elder son Marcus did (Marcus was in the kitchen at the time because he likes watching Anni. Well he *is* fifteen now). What my son said can be taken as gospel, because despite him wanting to be a solicitor when he grows up I have yet to find him out in a lie.

The thing is that although your directions may be clear to all but the most stupid of English people they are not at all clear to a not very bright Norwegian au pair who doesn't understand much

195

English, and very probably not clear to many more not very bright foreigners too - I'm thinking here of the hordes of Poles and other East Europeans who have descended on us recently - so with that in mind I think it might be prudent if you were to alter your directions from 'throw in a small can of tuna to 'throw in the *contents* of a small can of tuna'; or even better '*carefully add* the *contents* of a small can of tuna', before a serious accident occurs.

Yours sincerely

T Ravenscroft (Mr)

*

Knorr

13 April

Mr T Ravenscroft
17 Lingland Road
New Mills
Cheshire

Dear Mr Ravenscroft

Thank you very much for your fabulous letter. I'm sorry to learn of your, or rather Anni's, recent experience with the Knorr Ragu For Kids pasta sauce. I can honestly say, this is the first time I have heard of this happening.

I'm sure you understand, when we propose an alternative serving suggestion we do intend that other products are fully removed from their packaging. We specifically use informal language on the pack to make the product more appealing to Kids and it seems as though the intended meaning got lost in translation. I have noted your comments and have forwarded them to the Knorr team for consideration.

I have also enclosed a voucher so you can purchase some more Ragu products. Hopefully these won't end up being assaulted by an unopened tin of tuna, and if they do, you can purchase spares with our compliments.

Might I also suggest encouraging you son, Marcus, to adopt a more advisory role in the kitchen. It may stop other instructions being distorted by translation, and in turn will give him more to me to spend with Anni.

Once again thank you for sharing your experience with us, and if you have any other queries or comments on any of our Unilever product then please do not hesitate to contact us again.

Yours sincerely

Amy Richmond
Careline Advisor

Enc
Generic UF Coupon £5

*

17 Lingland Road
New Mills
CHESHIRE

16th April

Amy Richards
Knorr Consumer Care
250 Gunnery Avenue
LONDON

Dear Amy Richmond

Believe me Amy, the state my son Marcus's hormones are in at the moment the only advice he is likely to give to Anni is to get her knickers down, and as far as spending more time with her is concerned it takes me all my time to keep the randy little bugger away from her as it is.

However, I must now return to the original incident in the kitchen involving your Ragu For Kids Tomato and Cheese pasta sauce. When the sauce was accidentally deposited on the floor it left a stain on several of our cream vinyl tiles. At the time I wasn't too concerned as I thought it would be a simple matter to remove it. How wrong I was, for despite trying everything I can think of the stain has stubbornly refused to be removed.

My wife is not best pleased with me about this - I had to tell her that I was responsible for it as she had already threatened to send Anni back to Norway if she did anything else stupid, after the incident with the cat and the vacuum cleaner - so I was wondering if you could help to get me out of the doghouse by recommending something that will remove Ragu For Kids Tomato and Cheese pasta sauce stains? I notice from your letter that Knorr is part of the Unilever group, which, if my memory serves me correctly, sprang from the Lever Bros soap company, so as experts on getting things clean you might be able to recommend something potent enough to do the job. And in view of the fact that you were in part responsible for the stain being there in the first place perhaps you could send me a free sample? Or another £5 voucher would do, whatever you think best.

Yours sincerely

T Ravenscroft (Mr)

*

Knorr

Ref 22918
25 April

Mr T Ravenscroft
17 Lingland Road
New Mills
Cheshire

Dear Mr Ravenscroft

Thank you once again for your letter with regards to Knorr Ragu For Kids, or now as the case may be the remains of said product. I'm sorry to learn that this product left a mark on your kitchen and hope that this can be resolved.

We use all natural ingredients in the Knorr Ragu For Kids range so I can only assume that it is a rather stubborn tomato that refuses to leave the tiles in your kitchen. Once again I apologise for any inconvenience this may have caused, or indeed may be causing.

After talking to my good friends in the Home and Personal Care department, I can advise you to try our Cif Power Cream Spray which is specially designed for kitchen use. This should not only clear up the stain, but also clear your current 'doghouse' status.

If you have any other queries with regards to Unilever products or require further advise on the issue, please do not hesitate to contact us at the above address. Please find enclosed a voucher to enable you to try Cif with our compliments.

Yours sincerely

Amy Richmond
Careline Advisor

Enc
277 HPC Coupon £5

*

17 Lingland Road
New Mills
CHESHIRE

1st May

Amy Richards
Knorr Consumer Care
250 Gunnery Avenue
LONDON

Dear Amy

I must say that Knorr is the most generous company I have ever dealt with, and I have dealt with a few. Twice I have written to you and on each occasion not only have you had the courtesy to write back to me promptly and efficiently but you have enclosed a voucher for £5. The only way this could have been bettered would have been if you had sent me £5 in cash, because to tell you the truth I don't buy Unilever products all that often (mind you I may not be familiar with them all, so maybe you can send me a complete list?). My wife says you are trying to bribe me so that I won't start blabbing about your pasta sauce ruining our kitchen tiles but I prefer to think you are a caring company, like Baxters Soup, who sent me a shed load of vouchers when I had cause to complain about their Cock-a-Leekie soup, and even as I write are considering my recipe for Cock of Puddings.

I tried your Cif Power Cream Spray as recommended by your good friends in the Home and Personal Care department, as you suggested, and it *almost* got rid of the stain. I say almost, in fact to my eyes the stain has disappeared altogether, but my wife swears she can still see something and she could be right because the woman has eyes a hawk would be proud of, believe me. Anyway I've moved the pedal bin over the alleged stain so it should no longer be a problem.

Yours sincerely

*

Knorr

Ref 22918
11 May

Mr T Ravenscroft
17 Lingland Road
New Mills
Cheshire

Dear Mr Ravenscroft

Thank you once again for your letter. I'm glad to hear that the Cif Power Spray worked, at least a little!

I'm sorry to learn that your wife thinks we are bribing you with vouchers, and can assure you that this is not the case. We merely want to rectify any issue, and address any comments you have or may have had with Unilever products. It is after all, what we are here for.

The following is a list of Unilever products available in the UK. Adez, Bertolli, Boursin, Bovril, Elmlea, Flora, Flora Omega 3 plus, Pro.activ, Hellman's, I Can't Believe It's Not Butter, Jif, Lipton Ice Tea, Marmite, Peperami, PG Tips, Pot Noodle, Scottish Blend, Slim Fast, Stork, Summer County, Carte D'Or, Cornetto, Magnum, Solero, Wall's and Vienetta, Brut, Dove, Impulse, Lux, Lynx, Mentadent, Pond's, Signal, Sunsilk, Sure, Timotei and Vaseline, Cif, Domestos and Persil.

You could also visit our website for more information. It has cleverly been called www.unilever.co.uk. The individual brands also have their own websites with even more information about specific ranges.

I'm aware that another voucher to try one of our products may be inappropriate. As a thank you for contacting us, I have taken the liberty of including an eclectic mix of Unilever items. I hope you enjoy these, and look forward to any comments you may have.

Yours sincerely

Amy Richmond
Careline Advisor

Enc
34 Colman's product range
108 Hellman's 'Your Sandwich Made It' book
128 Marmite – Set of Beer Mats
114 ICBINB! Halloween Face Paint Pack

*

17 Lingland Road
New Mills
CHESHIRE

18th May

Amy Richards
Knorr Consumer Care
250 Gunnery Avenue
LONDON

Dear Amy

Thank you for the many gifts, which far from allaying my wife's suspicions that you are bribing me have only served to increase them. But then she is a suspicious woman, as I have sometimes found to my cost, and it is only a matter of time before she makes good her threat to send Anni back to Norway.

With the £10 worth of vouchers you have sent thus far I purchased another Cif Power Cream Spray (in the hope that it would work better than the previous one; it didn't, so the pedal bin will have to remain where it is for the time being), a packet of I Can't Believe It's Not Butter (I can, by the way), a packet of Boursin, a jar of Marmite, a jar of Hellmann's Mayonnaise, two packets of Peperami, a sachet of Slimfast and a jar of Vaseline. I then sliced a baguette in half, spread the I Can't Believe It's Not Butter on it, thought better of it, scraped it off and spread Lurpak butter on it instead, then piled on the Peperami, all the Boursin, the sachet of Slimfast, half the Marmite, two generous dollops of the Hellmann's Mayonnaise and a teaspoonful of Vaseline.

My idea is that although this very tasty sandwich contains a host of fattening foods they will be neutralized by the Slimfast, giving a sandwich that is not only extremely tasty but also non-fattening. (You might question the inclusion of Vaseline but apart from adding a certain *je ne sais quoi* to a sandwich it helps it to slip down, and is an absolute must with bacon or sausage and oven chips).

204

I intend to enter this sandwich for your next 'Your Sandwich Made It!' book. It feels like a winner to me.

Yours sincerely

T Ravenscroft (Mr)

****

During the course of writing this book, in addition to the items sent by Knorr and various samples of foods sent by other companies I received £127 in vouchers, plus a cheque for £10 from Bernard Matthews. Now I'm not suggesting for one moment that you should make up complaints in order to benefit from the largesse of these companies, but....?

Printed in Great Britain
by Amazon

62573361R00119